1.50

G000168483

Kirklees
Metropoltan
Council

Libraries and Museums Service

Huddersfield HD1 2SU
Tel: Hudd. 21356

19. JUN 80

29. [illegible] 80

WITHDRAWN

B

This book should be returned to the library from which it was borrowed on or before the latest date stamped above.

If not required by another borrower, the loan period may be extended for a further four weeks by post, telephone or personal visit. No more than three renewals permitted.

225 537 002

Landscape With Weeds

Landscape With Weeds

GRAHAM ROSE

Sunday Times Gardening Correspondent

ELM TREE BOOKS . LONDON

Acknowledgements

My sincere thanks are due to Bobby, Grace, Doff and Liesi who suffered most; Terry Carroll and the slaves who worked hardest; Willa Hancock who made the manuscript legible and especially to Stephen Wood who made it readable.

KIRKLEES LIBRARIES & MUSEUMS
ACC. No. 225 537 002
CLASS 635·092
DEPT. B
CHECKED HT

First published in Great Britain 1980
by Elm Tree Books/Hamish Hamilton Ltd
Garden House 57/59 Long Acre WC2E 9JZ

Copyright © 1980 by Graham Rose

British Library Cataloguing in Publication Data

Rose, Graham John
Landscape with weeds.
1. Landscape gardening — England — Faringdon
I. Title
712'.6'0924 SB477.G7

ISBN 0 241 10353 3

Printed in Great Britain by Bristol Typesetting Co Ltd,
Barton Manor, St Philips, Bristol

Illustrations

Foreword

What's so special about Graham Rose? I'll tell you. He has made a very special garden—taking about eight years to do it. But how did he make it? *He* didn't. Like the Romans he enlisted slave labour; but, unlike the Romans, libations of food and wine are fed to the slaves to keep them submissive and pliant. He enlists—and how did he ever find them? I've lived in the country for fifty years and I know the difficulties—'reliable', 'hardworking' craftsmen; and he only has weekends to recruit them in.

Elms die on him but improve his view. Rabbits invade him but are soon subjected to trigger-mortis—or are they?

Through all these wonders and vicissitudes, he proceeds on his unflappable way parading some most comical country characters and manages, rather craftily, to insert, here and there, very wise horticultural hints so that by the end of this enjoyable book you have learned, effortlessly and with much sugaring of the pill, a whole lot of garden lore and procedures.

In short, you cannot wait to know what happened and you are learning painlessly in the meantime. I will not keep you from Mr Rose any longer.

CYRIL FLETCHER

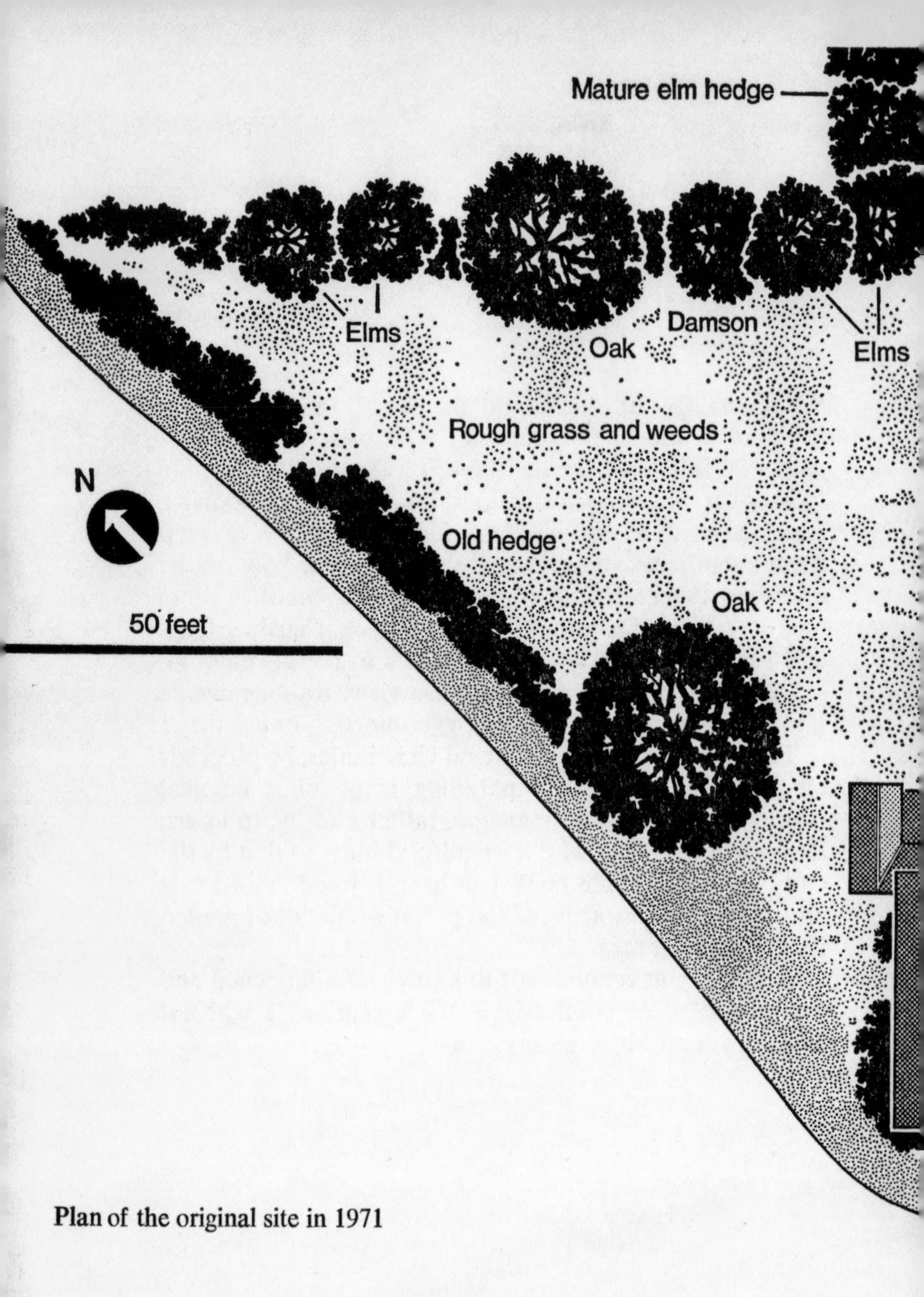

Plan of the original site in 1971

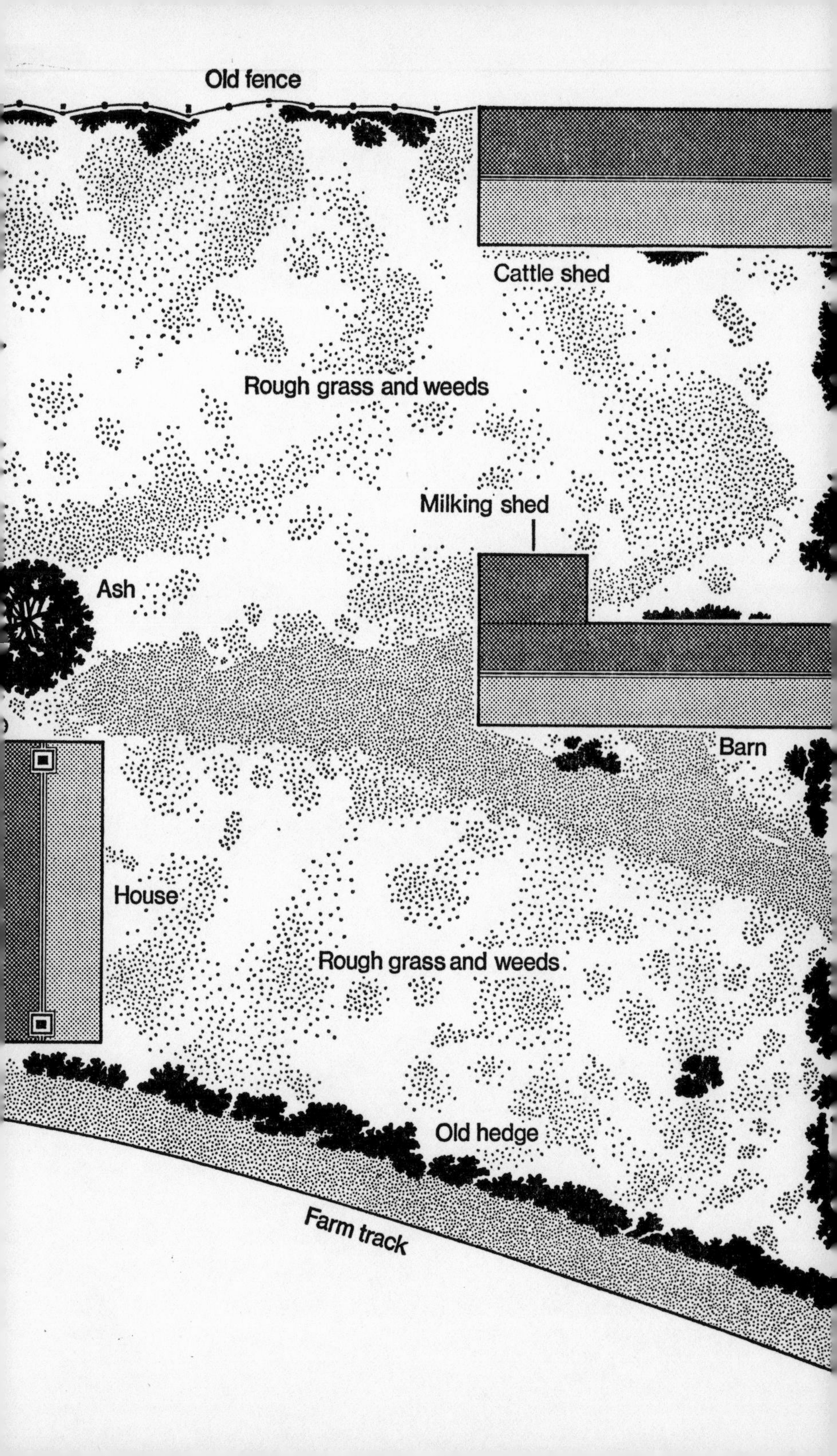
Old fence
Cattle shed
Rough grass and weeds
Milking shed
Ash
Barn
House
Rough grass and weeds
Old hedge
Farm track

Chapter One

Pushing open the cellar door, Martyn switched on the torch. The still, black surface of water which reflected the beam of light nearly reached the top of the steps. Doff and I were horrified. 'That's a good sign,' said Martyn cheerily. 'Never be short of water for the garden.'

Doff was clearly very dubious. Even in January after a damp autumn it was difficult to understand why a house poised so near the crest of a hill should have an inundated cellar. Martyn understood. 'This one has her boots firmly shuffled into the spring line. Probably why they built her here in the first place.'

Doff was less curious about the motivation of the nineteenth-century builders than about the practicalities wives must face. 'But the damp?' she asked anxiously.

Martyn Tucker has a delightful, almost arrogant, way of dismissing the mundane. 'No problem at all. Make it into an island. Dig an eight-foot ditch round the perimeter and fill it with gravel so that the water supply flows round it and off down the hill.'

'Just like that,' his wife, Imogen, said, gesturing with her hands as though proffering a pre-packed solution. Her neon bright smile was displayed to dismiss the hours of drudgery she had suffered while participating in Martyn's past projects.

He had been equally confident in the bedroom while Doff was sourly eyeing the tumbling ceiling plaster. 'That's a stroke of luck,' he cried. 'Small bore pipes to carry Calor gas to the lights. You could camp in here very comfortably while doing-up the rest.'

It had become clear that Martyn's passion for 'doing up' was boundless. Every time we met him he seemed to have shifted homes in order to embark upon a further, even more ambitious, restoration.

His enthusiasm was infectious. Despite the wet cellar, the general disrepair and the continuous roar of the prototype Concorde landing and taking off at the RAF base just over the hill, we began to feel that the house had much in its favour.

Its situation was certainly splendid. Just before dark in the curdy pink light of that winter Saturday evening in 1971 we peered into the secretive folds of the Cotswolds to the north-west. To the south and east lay the moist pastures and cosy villages of that area of the upper Thames valley so loved by William Morris.

The stone walls of the house seemed sound and immovable. The roof looked as if it would keep out water when a few tiles had been replaced. Three-quarters of an acre of surrounding meadow were available to establish a garden. And the fine barn in matching stone could, as Martyn promptly pointed out, 'be easily linked to the house to make a tremendous studio for parties'. There was nothing Martyn liked more, after a hard day's 'doing-up ', than a party.

Martyn's enthusiasm and my depression at having lost two attractive houses in Dutch auctions during the previous three months made a powerful combination. I felt we should take it. But I could see that Doff, a tremendously experienced and competent 'doer-up' herself, still had a doubt.

'It's the name,' she said. 'How can anybody live in a house called Lye Down?'

'Well, call it Hill House for heaven's sake,' Martyn snorted impatiently, appalled by the idea that a chance to advise on so much doing-up should be lost to a triviality like a name.

When we reached the estate agent's office it was closed; so I dropped the key through the letter box. We would make our decision next day and I would ring early on Monday morning. I was relieved not to have to face the pompous young clerk twice in one day. Rural properties fit for modernization were becoming scarce in central southern England. None of them were going for a song any more, which enabled a young clerk with a windsor knotted tie and a suit from Lord John to provide access to them with the remote aplomb of a cardinal bestowing a blessing.

Sadly, the façade hid almost complete ignorance. The only characteristic of any property which he understood was its price. Questions about access to main drainage, soil type, or the availability of such services as electricity or water were dismissed with a testy 'No idea'.

However, there was a trace of genuine pleasure in his voice when he replied to my offer to buy Lye Down on Monday morning: 'Afraid it's gone.'

Oh. Had he anything else to offer?

'Nothing you would be interested in. There's a Georgian rectory at £47,000. Not quite what you are seeking, I imagine?'

His idea of what I was seeking was, I knew, rather vague, but this time I had to admit he was quite right. I tried to sting him back.

'I was under the impression that you specialized in older properties in this district. You don't seem to offer much of a choice.'

Pitiful really. He treated it with the contempt it deserved. 'Tremendous demand, you know.' The hauteur implied that the scarcity was something which he had been clever enough to create himself. 'Just nothing at present which falls within your range.'

'Absolutely nothing? Not even an old barn or something?' I insisted.

'Well, of course, if you want to involve yourself in that sort of bother and expense, we have got a total ruin in the Vale of the White Horse, but I'm afraid that you might consider even the price of that a shade over the top.' He was becoming impatient. I thanked him curtly and, very depressed, put down the phone.

Martyn and Imogen swept away the depression with gusts of enthusiasm when I rang to tell them the news. They knew the ruin they said. 'Sensational view! We tried to buy it two years ago,' Imogen explained.

'Terrible load of grot, total ruin, half the roof gone, timber rotted—it's got a fantastic potential. Absolutely right for doing-up,' Martyn carolled. 'Get back down here right away.'

Galvanized, I was soon speeding away from London down the M4 and before lunchtime I'd wriggled my way across the Berkshire Downs, passed the flank of the White Horse and arrived in the Vale.

Surveying the ruined farmstead, I decided that this time Martyn's mania for doing-up had gone too far.

The house looked blind. All the windows had been blocked up with ragged hardboard to protect the remaining glass. The provision of the key had been an empty estate agent's gesture —I could easily have climbed in through the gaping roof. Here, too, water was no problem. As I groped my way through the half-light inside, slithering on the slimy stone-flagged floor and trying not to trip over the compost of falling ceiling plaster and rotting laths, it started to rain and the walls began to run with water. I had to hurry back to the car to avoid being drenched. It was clear that anyone forced to spend more than half an hour in the house would die of exposure.

I was smoking angrily contemplating Martyn's perfidy when he splashed his way up the 300-yard farm track from the road and slid to a halt.

'Look at the marvellous outbuildings,' he extolled. The decrepit remnants of a barn door lurched from one hinge like a broken wing. Part of a wall was tumbling into the man-high nettles. The flapping, corroded, corrugated iron roof of a six-bay cattle-shed made melancholy music in the wind.

While I ruminated pessimistically, Martyn shuffled urgently about the muddy surrounds. In his gumboots and sheepskin coat he looked like a tank commander surveying the devastation after a successful attack. Nothing could staunch the flow of encouraging advice. 'That roof can be fixed with no bother at all. Just rip down those back gable ends and make it into a giant lean-to.'

'Of course, this monstrous porch will have to go,' he said, thumping it hard with his boot as he passed to see if it could go immediately. He charged inside. The equally monstrous 1930s tiled fireplace in the dining-room infuriated him.

'Why did they do it?' he ranted as he rushed outside again. Returning seconds later with a short crowbar, he began to wrench the stylized sunset from the wall.

Freed from the car along with the crowbar, Martyn's Weimarana, Pad, barked enthusiastically.

'There, I knew it,' he declared triumphantly. His eyes shone as he pointed gleefully through the cloud of cement dust. 'There's always something worth groping for.'

And, indeed, the splendid old Victorian cast-iron fireplace with a wheat and bindweed motif which he had revealed was the first remotely worthwhile thing I'd seen since I arrived.

A few more minutes of urgent and noisy activity with the crowbar enabled Martyn to reveal further treasures. Ripping the top off the windowledges, he discovered solid wooden sash shutters. Wrenching away some worm-eaten cupboards, he found the former window bays in the walls of the eighteenth-century section of the house. Making the stone flags of the floor ring with a bounce of his bar, he chortled with delight.

'No need for you to spend a fortune on York stone slabs when you want to pave your yard. This lot is worth its weight in gold.'

By the time he'd finished his prodding, probing and thumping, he was convinced. 'It's a snip,' he said. 'Grab it while you can.' I wasn't sure whether I had any option. He had done so much damage that I thought I'd probably have to buy it.

As we came out of the house, the rain stopped and the sky cleared. Sensing that my resolve was weakening, Martyn played his trump card. He dug his heel into the soil between the massive tufts of cocksfoot grass.

'Ferruginous sand,' he declared. 'Next to our Greensand further up the hill, that's some of the best growing soil in England. It's a bastard to work: sticky as hell when wet and sets like rock when it's dry. But if you catch it right and handle it carefully, it will grow almost anything.'

As Martyn well knew, we were looking primarily for land to make a garden rather than a house to make a home. However resistant I might be to party potential and doing-up opportunities, I was unlikely to fail to appreciate the importance of good soil.

'Mind you,' he said, gesturing towards the south-west, 'you'll have to make some garden to match that.' Looking out over the shallow valley to the White Horse, clearly visible on the far side, I had to agree with him. Gazing round at the desolate frost-scorched thicket of brambles and nettles destined to become our garden, I realized that I was about to invest in a landscape with weeds.

Chapter Two

After the months spent looking for a house, our first job now that we had found one was to hide it. Some houses are beautiful enough to be an asset to the garden; most, like ours, need at least some cosmetic treatment.

It was late spring before we exchanged contracts and took possession. By then, the hedgerows and trees were covered with a froth of softening foliage and the couch grass was sprouting everywhere. But the house was as bleak as it had been in January. The original eighteenth-century part, a farmhouse with picturesque windows and mellow stone walls, was almost invisible from the garden, hidden by the larger Victorian addition. Big white shutters on the ground-floor windows and a coat of white paint on the front door had helped a little, breaking the monotony of the large areas of nondescript brick. But every time we drove up the track, that brick façade seemed to dominate.

'Doing-up' was just one of the Tucker family talents. Martyn's quiet thoughtful brother, Mike, ran the retail side of a nursery business founded by their great-grandfather and continued by their famous father, John, in the Vale. Mike was the expert in covering-up. Impressing upon him the urgency of the task of hiding our bricks, I asked him for advice on the most suitable plants for the job.

'Anything fast will do,' I said.

With an air of disappointed resignation, Mike held up an admonitory finger. Another of these amateur gardeners. Always so impatient. 'Now, now, now. Just hold on a minute. Not so fast.'

In retrospect, that was the gesture and those were the words, uttered with some indignation, which have most frequently prefaced our encounters since that day seven years ago.

'Fast's all right, but don't forget you've got to live with the bloomin' result.'

I realize now that Mike doesn't employ this technique simply to prevent planting errors. Like most nurserymen, he has little time or land left for pleasure gardening. But he chose his profession out of love and can't resist gardening vicariously. By making his customers think again and urging them to be both more thoughtful and ambitious in their planning, he can do a little gardening himself. He draws attention to more appropriate, interesting or attractive subjects, prevails upon the innocent to plant them and then, after a season or two, takes pleasure in popping round to inspect their progress.

New gardeners should be encouraged to discover and rely on experienced nurserymen like Mike. They should also be warned. Like cunning drug-pushers, they gently wean the beginner from the cheap and commonplace which nurserymen find boring, on to the rare and exotic varieties which, while fascinating, can also be expensive. Quite heartless in the way they sponsor gardening fanaticism, good nurserymen can contemplate their clients' ragged under-nourished children, or the prospect of such profligacy leading to divorce, without even a twinge of conscience as they persuade their poor addicts to carry away yet another costly gem 'which will look perfect when planted near that wall'.

Perhaps the most irritating habit of the nurserymen who become really familiar with your garden is the way in which they will come to use it as a source of stock plants. Knowing that you owe them many favours for past kindnesses ('Go on then, take those,' they say when filling your car boot with valuable old seed boxes or loads of used pots in response to your cadging, 'I wonder if . . .?'), nurserymen pillage your beds and shrubberies without compunction. Apart from some freshly turned soil or an impression that the balance of a plant has slightly changed, they are so stealthy that you are usually quite unaware of the thefts. Sometimes they will pop round just after dawn on a Sunday or very late at night—if you are lucky you might just catch them, like the fairies at the bottom of the garden, with their sap-stained secateurs. Sometimes you see them, over a spoonful of soup, as they tap on the dining-room window: 'Let down by a supplier—he sent the white variety and the client ordered the pink and is hopping mad, so I just took a few root cuttings from yours.'

It is obvious that to be a successful nurseryman able to supply even the most uncommon plants at a moment's notice involves the most prodigious feat of memory. I am convinced that, even locked in a darkened room, Mike Tucker could list the location of every plant in our garden to within a centimetre.

But then that's not surprising, for he has supplied most of them. And, frequently, as on that first encounter, the transaction has begun with the gruff command: 'Come and look at this.'

'Be sure to show him the Belgica,' said Margaret, his mother, as I followed Mike out of the office in search of a solution to my cover-up problem. 'And I expect after you've finished with him he'll need a cup of tea,' she added hospitably.

Surrounding her house, less than a minute's walk away from the nursery-sales area, Margaret has created a trap from which few customers can have escaped empty-handed—one of the most beautiful medium-sized gardens in England. It's a series of billowing shrubberies and shrub borders between which the visitor wanders on smoothly-clipped walks. The highest points are formed by maturing trees, as carefully chosen for their all-seasons display of bark, foliage and blossom as are the smaller shrubs.

The areas beneath the densest shade provide a wonderful environment for an incomparable collection of shade- and cool-loving plants. In the sunnier spots, where the shrubbery foliage peters out, there is a yard or two of carefully chosen perennial herbaceous plants. These border edges contain the one essential ingredient in every garden: the element of surprise. Just when you have become slightly wistful, having noticed that a shrub peony is fading, you start with joy on taking the next step—to discover that a previously hidden dwarf lilac is coming into bloom.

But Margaret's garden is an expensive pleasure—it must have cost me a fortune over the years. The element of surprise may charm the casual visitor; it can also charm the wallet out of the pocket of the jaded gardener who has a garden to create from nothing and who has spent too long poring over books and catalogues. Mike leads you into the trap which Margaret has set, shows you something at its very best in a splendid location, and knows that nothing less can then satisfy you. Of course, when the shrubs are delivered, you have to make do with considerably less: less shrub (Margaret's is at its peak, yours is several years away from it), and a less splendid location.

Before we got back for tea, Mike didn't forget to show me the magnificent Lonicera Belgica—early Dutch honeysuckle—which was just starting to show the reddish-purple, heavily scented blooms.

I have learned to cherish tea with Margaret and Mike. It is like a gardening master class. Both possess the ability to home in on the essence of a gardening problem; both attack the problem in different ways. To the pupil, the cumulative effect is fascinating.

Mike has a brooding intellectual approach. He sips his tea and muses quietly about fundamental disciplines—the location of the site, the type and state of the soil, the aspect, the degree of shelter, the plants in the vicinity—before beginning to select potential candidates from his endless mental catalogue. Margaret thinks aloud. Like a joyful, fast-working, water-colour painter, she sketches lightning mental pictures from a palette of stems, foliage and flowers. She, like all great plastic artists, thinks effortlessly in three dimensions, understanding just how plants will relate to each other when planted in the garden and while maturing.

It took several cups of tea to sort out my cladding problem.

The Belgica honeysuckle was finally rejected in favour of Lonicera japonica for a prime site on the southern wall of the house. Because this is an evergreen form of honeysuckle, it will hide the brick even in winter. As a concession to my impatience, the Tuckers let me put a Clematis montana on the same façade. Although this loses its leaf in winter, it is such a rampant grower and produces so much tangled woody stem so quickly that it even provides useful cover when it is bare. It is heartening, too, to grow something which produces such an extensive blanket of pale pink stars so soon after it is planted.

To make sure there were roses round the door as quickly as possible, we chose a rapidly-climbing version of the vermilion Superstar.

On the less exposed walls of the house, I put up with slower growers. On the west side, the elegant climbing lacecap Hydrangea petiolaris would go near the front of the house, in the hope that ultimately its greenish-white flowers could be led round the corner to provide additional cover on the façade. Further back, we put a Wisteria sinensis—because every house should have one. For the northern and eastern faces, Winter Jasmine—Jasminum nudiflorum (bright-yellow flowers on naked stems in winter) and the spectacular variegated ivy, Gloire de Marengo.

Which left the outbuildings. The barn had a rather nice wall—six feet of stone and then brick up to the eaves—half of it would make a good background to the taller plants in an herbaceous bed, with just one rambling New Dawn rose to break up the other half.

The cattle-shed was another matter altogether. From the house, it offered a delightful prospect of wooden supports holding up a nasty blue corrugated iron-roof. A major difficulty? Elsewhere, perhaps, but well within the problem-solving capabilities of Tea at the Tuckers. The answer was wire and climbers. Up the wooden supports we would grow more Gloire de Marengo ivy. Then we would put strips of chicken wire from the eaves up to the ridge of the roof and let the ivy climb all over the corrugated iron. Strips of wire would also support Van Fleet and Schoolgirl climbing roses, a Russian vine, another evergreen honeysuckle, Clematis montana, and a startling purple Clematis jackmanii.

The ugly blue roof would soon disappear under a thick thatch of foliage and flowers. Eventually, when the metal corrodes away, the shed will have a splendid self-supporting, living roof. An important lesson for all gardeners: if you cover a problem up, it *might* go away.

As I left the Tuckers', I congratulated myself on a successful afternoon's work. I had dealt decisively with an urgent problem. All I'd got left to do was pay for what I'd ordered, plant them out—and then wait a few years.

Chapter Three

I had planted the first shrubs against the wall just as Mike had commanded. 'Get them going as soon as you can, so that they can start to establish—you can produce a garden later by working away from the walls. And for goodness sake give them a decent home.'

If Martyn had been enthusiastic about the land and building on that first visit, Mike had been positively ecstatic about the cattle dung. 'Wonderful, wonderful,' he cried, plunging his hands into eighteen-inches of manure dropped on the floor of the cattle-shed by wintering beasts twenty years earlier. 'You'd go a long way to find an asset like that.'

I was already realizing the asset. I had dug holes twice as deep and twice as wide as the root balls of the shrubs, probed the bottom of each hole with a fork and crowbar and then floored them with a rich mixture of the dung and soil, just as Mike had prescribed. Before planting the shrubs and back-filling with weed-free soil, I'd filled the holes with water and allowed them to drain.

I was returning with another can of water from the stand-pipe we'd got working in the kitchen to provide the final 'water-in', when I saw Mrs Beastly-Trout standing in front of her Land Rover staring angrily at the ground.

She merely 'humphed' in reply to my welcoming 'Good Morning' and continued to eye sourly two bedraggled rows of well-trodden perennial plants which I'd fetched from our last garden and simply thrown into a temporary trench until I decided where to plant them. She obviously thought that was my idea of a flowerbed.

'Can I help at all?' I proffered.

It was a fatuous question. How could anyone in torn, cement-splattered jeans and a fraying St Michael pullover have assisted someone with so grand a Sherlock Holmes tweed hat. She didn't bother to reply and simply began muttering to what had obviously been a malign deity. 'Bin usin' this patch to park the horsebox for the last five years.'

When I glanced at her daughter, Francesca, an agreeable, if toothy girl in flawless white jodhpurs and well-boned boots, I could see from the way she was busily fondling her horse that she was as embarrassed as I was.

I suppose I ought to have realized that I was involuntarily playing host to the Vale's answer to Pat Smythe.

'Use it as often as you please—it will be months before the garden is arranged,' I said, trying to be good-neighbourly.

She glanced round at the devastation created by the laying of water mains and digging of the septic tank and drainage ditches. She was very displeased. Barely acknowledging my gesture, she snapped her fingers at Francesca and said imperiously, 'Better fetch him out.'

Feeling superfluous and somewhat piqued, I lumbered back to the wall to begin watering but by the time I'd slowly emptied the first can my temper had abated. Watching the loose soil suck down to form a slight depression about the stems as the water drained away, I felt pleased with myself for having so carefully followed Mike's advice. 'Never flirt when you are watering. Either saturate or leave well alone. It's the most vital job in the garden and so many people leave it to children.' The basin formed round the stem would help to retain water later in the season, he had explained, while confirming that if you can get most trees and shrubs through their first year by keeping their roots nice and moist, they can usually be ignored from then on.

'Watch the clematis though—she likes very damp feet,' he'd added.

As I wandered around looking for a decent lump of rock to put over the clematis roots to retain moisture, I reflected that the Beastly-Trout problem was probably not just a local phenomenon. Wherever land is poorly fenced, or unfenced, in town or country, it tends to become a public thoroughfare.

Custom leads the locals to feel that they have proprietary rights. Anyone buying the land and wanting to create a bit of privacy is bound to face unpopularity—they will always be blocking someone's short-cut to the bus stop or fencing off somebody's parking space.

My thoughts were interrupted by a series of noisy commands from the local opposition to private enclosure—these indicated that the Beastly-Trout cavalcade was, after the traditional interminable period of girth-tightening and harness-fidgeting, ready to move off. However, thanks to the wonderful Gerhart, the cavalcade moved off very swiftly indeed, and, after that day's outing, never reappeared.

Gerhart's sunny personality and his talents as a builder resulted from the perfect fusion of two cultures. A strong work ethic, boundless energy and Gothic earnestness derived from his German father blended happily with the easygoing Englishness of his mother. His parents had met when his prisoner-of-war father had been trusted to work on a farm near Newbury and had come to like Britain enough to decide to stay on after the fighting had ended.

We were pleasantly surprised by Gerhart's estimate for the major structural changes needed to make the house habitable: it undercut all the other estimates by almost £1,500. We were also slightly concerned as to how he could do the work so cheaply, especially when people mentioned the phrase 'jerry-built'.

The answer, we soon discovered, was simple. Gerhart didn't walk. Apparently he couldn't. He could only run—everywhere, all the time. Even when pushing a huge barrow-load of wet concrete.

He had just dumped one such load in the house and was sprinting out of the back door to get another, balancing the wheel of the barrow on a narrow plank runway, when he rather suddenly met Francesca Beastly-Trout and her horse. In his efforts to avoid the horse, Gerhart had to swing his barrow off the runway. The barrow tipped over and went flying, closely followed by Gerhart and a string of oaths.

Mrs Beastly-Trout's scream of 'Idiot' rang back from the piles of building blocks and bricks like a howitzer report. And, coupled with the sound of the crashing barrow, it galvanized Francesca's 16.2 show-jumper into a nervous lurch between the parked cars and an instant gallop up the farm track.

'Push your feet forward and pull him up. Sit down and feet forward! Feet forward!' yelled Mrs Beastly-Trout bustling after them.

Climbing slowly to his feet, Gerhart began to laugh convulsively. 'I told you,' he cried, still shaking. 'You really will have to put up a fence!'

The need to ensure our privacy became more urgent as the weather improved. During the summer, more and more of our friends from London turned up at weekends to work in the garden. We called them 'the slaves'. They didn't seem to mind.

It wasn't that our slaves couldn't tolerate the locals laughing at their efforts. The problem was that topless sunbathing had swept north that year from St Tropez and had reached the Vale of the White Horse. The little band of nubile slaves, who liked to relax after their labours without their bikini tops, was getting insufficient protection from the hedge, and, in consequence, was causing a major traffic problem on the farm track.

It was the traffic I'd noticed first. Normally, perhaps twice a week, a tractor would pass drawing a trailer loaded with such farming paraphernalia as bundles of barbed-wire or piles of fence-posts. It usually bounced by so quickly that the driver barely had time to acknowledge our greeting with a brief wave from inside the closed cab.

As the weather warmed up, it was understandable that the drivers should hold open the cab doors with binder-twine or even that they should lean out to catch the breeze as they drove. But their business seemed to have become less urgent. Their engines puttered gently instead of roaring as they cruised sedately past our garden. Why, I wondered, did they need to pay so many more visits to the upper fields? The hay had, I knew, already been carted and the barley wasn't ready to be cut. The trailers seemed strangely bare. Two empty sacks which could easily have been carried on the handlebars of a bicycle were on one occasion the only obvious freight. They were still there when the tractor returned, only minutes later!

I discovered the answer to this agricultural puzzle by accident. I had taken a ladder out on to the farm track to prune the top of one of the willows in what remained of the hedge. As I climbed the steps I discovered that, just at tractor level, the perspective changed: there, laid out in a line like seals basking on a rock, surrounded by mud and builders' rubble, were half a dozen topless sunbathers.

I hadn't given more than a moment's thought to the problem of fencing after I—or rather Gerhart—had got rid of the Beastly-Trout entourage. But this less obtrusive invasion of our privacy threatened serious long-term consequences. The farm track, our only means of access to the house, couldn't take the new level of tractor traffic for long—it was already causing untold suffering to our car, grown soft and fat on London traffic jams and the gentle undulations of the M4. More important, I had my reputation in the district to worry about. Having previously suffered from country conservatism, I was concerned about local reaction to our semi-nudist colony: we had to continue to live in the Vale when the slaves had driven, red-busted, home.

Most important of all, however, I had to look after the interests of my slaves. It occurred to me that some of the female slaves might not come if they couldn't get in a few hours' sunbathing in privacy. And if they didn't come, neither would their husbands and boyfriends. And I needed my slaves; so I resolved to try and think of a way of thickening the hedge in the very near future.

There was no doubt that, whatever Mike might think, my slaves were an even greater asset than the pile of ancient cow dung in the cattle-shed; for they didn't have to be driven to their heroic tasks—they drove themselves down the M4 and volunteered. The whole idea of volunteer slaves was a revolutionary concept and, like most revolutions, it was born of frustration.

People had taken our previous downland house and garden for granted. Escaping from their offices, laboratories, studios and libraries in London, they had refuged there, winter and summer alike. Huge lumps of sirloin beef from Mr Mountjoy in Marylebone, Gorgonzola and Stilton from Paxtons in Jermyn Street, pâté from Fortnums or Harrods, salmon from Mr Green at Crouch End, cases of Burgundy from Dolomore in Paddington Green had, over the years, been ferried into Berkshire and brandished like passports at our gate. When we left that chalkland paradise, they were suddenly frustrated. Instead of our brisk breezes, they were left to breathe the ethyl lead-filled air of town. Like ordinary citizens, they had to face the long Saturday and Sunday queues for cinemas and fight their way to tables in expensive crowded restaurants.

Their plight was lamentable and when it became quite intolerable, they began to make discreet inquiries about our progress in the Vale.

In reply to our 'It's a perfect ruin. Months of work yet', the more desperate among them suggested that they'd 'like to help'.

Looking at the softness of their white bibliophile hands and remembering the luxury and comfort of their homes, we dissented vigorously. 'No, no,' we said. 'We simply couldn't. Conditions are too awful. Next year, perhaps.'

It worked as well as Tom Sawyer's reluctance to allow the boys to wield the brush. So many of them turned up the next Saturday that we hardly knew how to arrange the parking of the cars.

'We are going to tear down that dreadful porch,' I announced, rather uncertainly, as I watched them struggling over the thirteen pairs of Wellingtons we discovered that it was essential to keep in the country. The wind was chilly and to keep them warm—and to protect the wholly inappropriate 'country gear' supplied by their tailors (which included a pair of genuine bison-hide shoes, price forty-six guineas)—we had dished out the ragged assortment of plastic macs, worn-out duffle coats and leaky golf jackets which had accumulated over the years. They looked as ferocious a bunch as the brick-laying team with Ivan Denisovich on the Gulag Archipelago.

'Get to it, then,' cried Cox, grabbing a sledge-hammer and beginning to pound away at the timber supports of the porch. Cox is a film director. With a cheer like an infants school breaking up for the holidays, all the other volunteers seized instruments of destruction and went to work.

I could see that there was no way of co-ordinating their activities, so I went back to digging holes along my boundary for the Lonicera hedging cuttings which Martyn had promised to provide.

By the time he turned up, the slaves' enthusiasm was waning. All the easy bits—the timber and corrugated iron—had been brought down. What they needed to lead their assault on the more obdurate sections of the structure was a maniac, someone who adored destruction, someone who saw demolition as delightful foreplay, the prelude to a serious bout of doing-up. Martyn's eyes glittered with excitement as he surveyed so much chaos. The challenge was irresistible; hurling aside his sheepskin coat, he tore a pickaxe from a startled actress's hand and led the attack.

I was absorbed in firming-in the Lonicera when I was disturbed by a slightly hurt voice. 'Say, Gray, haven't you got some gardening for me. Gardening's more in my line, you know.' It was Faber. I could tell he wanted to lay out a path.

In our previous garden he had become *the* expert on paths. He liked paths because they were such obvious features—he could quickly survey his own progress and, once they were established, he could proudly point them out to everyone. Happily he was very good at them; no one could strike a better level, keep to a straighter line or mark out a more telling and appropriate curve. Since we had no paths whatever, I handed him a spade, two sticks and some twine and pointed to the hummocky land between the house and the barn. 'A path there would be useful,' I said.

Getting back to the Lonicera, I proudly considered my managerial skills. I had quickly discovered that to get the best results from a team like mine, there is one simple rule: you must find out what they enjoy, and what they are good at, and let them do that. Set on their course, they can be safely ignored.

The second simple rule is that they can never be safely ignored. It took me a little longer—a day, in fact—to discover that slaves must always be watched from afar if disaster is to be avoided. Once land is planted, a slave who loves weeding can throw away hundreds of costly plants. A crowded mixed bed of groundsel, chickweed and seedling annual flowers can, within an hour, become a neat bed of beautifully spaced groundsel or chickweed. And tender seedling annuals which have just begun to establish nice sturdy roots take very unkindly to being brutally torn up and confined to the bottom of a rubbish heap. Training for such complex tasks and discreet supervision is obviously necessary.

As I also discovered on that first self-help day, a tiny,

newly planted rosemary bush won't thrive if all its foliage is used to perfume the smoke and flavour the meat of a rack of lamb. Barbecuing that joint was the less vigorous task quickly selected by the feebler members of the team to rest muscles, tired from demolition work. As soon as they had recovered enough worm-eaten timber from the porch to start a fire, they had dropped their tools and begun to indulge in pyrotechnics.

Sadly, I was working behind a hedge when the fire finally caught. I had become increasingly aware of the scornful laughter caused by the failures of several self-styled fire-lighting experts. But I only emerged, attracted by the whoop of joy when someone threw a jet of paraffin on to a few dying embers and turned the fire into a roaring conflagration, in time to witness the disaster.

The branches of the noble ash tree under which they had piled their timber had seemed high and remote. But I could see that, fed by the paraffin, the flames were already beginning to shrivel the leaves. Even a fireman would have had difficulty in preventing further damage and I had to stand impotently by as several attractive fronds sizzled and withered.

They looked a bit crestfallen and fell quiet as I rebuked them. 'Lesson number one in the camper's manual: never light a fire beneath a tree.'

When it was cooked, they sheepishly offered me some of the most delectable morsels as a gesture of peace. I accepted gladly but have often reflected on how costly that meal was. The tree still looks unbalanced and bears the scars of cooking to this day.

While guzzling the delicious lamb and swilling back the accompanying wine, I realized why the man who founded the Club Méditerranée was so successful. Sophisticated city folk long for the simpler life. But it's the notion not the reality which really attracts them.

Make them sleep in a bare straw thatched hut and walk miles barefoot like pilgrims across hot sand to the sanitation centres. But make sure that they are scrupulously clean when they get there. And, above all, feed them like lions because their jaded urban appetites will recover rapidly in wholesome fresh air.

Strewn around the fire in their bizarre garb, sitting on drums of bitumen, sacks of cement or piles of building blocks with their faces streaked with soot and cement dust, my slaves all looked wonderfully satisfied with their morning's work and its culinary reward.

'This is just like Club Med,' I said, remembering a marvellous lamb barbecue in the Atlas Mountains.

'Hellish Holidays, you mean,' some wit retorted, rubbing hard at the muscles of his lower back which had begun to twinge painfully.

The name stuck.

Chapter Four

Work on the house was still progressing at running pace—Gerhart hadn't slowed up at all. We now had bedrooms, even a bathroom. I was almost pleased.

It wasn't that I couldn't appreciate the importance of making the house habitable—my labour force would, after all, welcome it. It was just that I was annoyed by the speed of Gerhart's relentless advance. I was jealous. He made all the effort put into *my* area of responsibility, the garden, look so futile. Gerhart was still making a mess, but it was a constructive mess. I still seemed to be making a mess, pure and simple, after four months.

One evening the unfairness of the whole thing struck me really hard. Fred and his mechanical digger were just leaving after—in that one day—digging all the holes and trenches that Gerhart would need. Two weeks' work for a dozen men! It was all very well for builders—*they* could hire people like Fred.

I rang Fred later that evening. Yes, he could come back next week.

As soon as he arrived I could tell that Fred was annoyed with me, but he was so gentle and kind that he hardly knew how to express anger. His appearance was also a handicap. The wide freckled cheeks were too bland to be mean. The blue eyes were so pale and soft they could never acquire the hard sparkle of wrath.

'If only you'd realized last week, it would have saved you a lot of money,' he said, tutting quietly as he gazed over the bucket of his wheezing mechanical digger. 'And me a lot of driving.'

It was a warm morning and the engine was so hot from its journey that thermals rising from the bonnet were distorting vision across the Vale.

I smiled apologetically and didn't say anything while he chewed hard on the stem of Timothy grass.

'Sixteen miles is a long way at four miles an hour.'

I glanced at my watch and realized that he must have left home shortly after 4 am.

As he spoke he kept removing and replacing the plate-like cap from his thicket of straw-blond hair. It was an action similar to the nervous tic of a test-match batsman striving to maintain concentration by following a routine. In Fred it betokened irritation. Whenever a large deep stone or tree root made trenching for a drain difficult, he would poise the nose of his digger arm delicately on the ground, climb down from the machine and peer into the hole. As the mysteries began to reveal themselves, he'd start to move his cap up and down.

I felt suitably guilty—like many innocent gardeners I had planned my operations badly. Still, at least I had discovered the rural night-people. They exist in every district but most gardeners are unaware of them. And sadly this ignorance leads to many hours of avoidable hard work.

The rural night-people are a tribe of itinerant one-man contractors. After working for the large civil engineering firms for years, they save enough money to pay the deposit on a secondhand earth mover of the type used on motorway workings or large building sites. They then work for up to twelve hours per day, seven days a week to maintain their hire-purchase instalments and their enviable independence. When necessary they form a team with an independent lorry driver who works on the same basis.

If they are very lucky and industrious, they can end up as building tycoons. One of them in our district, who bought his machine after leaving the RAF, retrained as a helicopter pilot at the government's expense and became the personal pilot to an Arabian Gulf Prince! But most of them, like Fred, just make a decent living.

To save valuable daylight for the work itself, they tend to

move their machines about in the dark. And, since the machines are slow and cumbersome, high roads are shunned in favour of the less frequented lanes. That is why the rural night-people seem so discreet. Long into the night, when even the poachers are dreaming and farm dogs and cockerels are too deeply asleep to be disturbed by the murmur of their engines, Britain's Freds, like a well co-ordinated brigade, thread their way through the landscape towards places where miracles will be performed the next morning.

It's a dangerous life. Fred has often had to jump clear as rural carousers returning late from Farmers' Club balls have crumpled their car bonnets against his stout digger bucket.

'It's a miracle me fuel hasn't gone up yet,' he reflected, pointing with his chewed grass at the self-sufficiency kit in his bucket: two steel drums of diesel oil and a snap box and tea flask. 'Mind you, they have shattered a couple of flasks and mangled me sandwiches on occasions.'

But it's not the brushes with careless motorists which cause the most anguish; Fred and his colleagues face far worse problems with night patrols of the police.

The machines which they drive are very costly and even secondhand models fetch high prices abroad. In consequence, the police are fighting a constant battle with an improbable type of criminal gang. These exporters are highly organized. Stealthily inspecting contractors' sites, they carefully note the engine numbers, makes and models of any machinery. Cabling these details to their agents abroad, they offer to sell the machines at attractive discounts. Once the order is confirmed, they arrange shipping space for the machines and satisfactory documentation. A few hours before the ship is due to sail, the machine is stolen from the site.

So when the police see valuable plant being driven along country lanes just before dawn, they do tend to stop and ask whether it's going, for instance, to Qatar, Bahrain or Port Harcourt.

But Fred's papers had been in order, he had got through, and now he was ready to change the face of the garden in a single day. After, that is, he had had his say.

'Pity you didn't plan it all ahead.'

I didn't feel that Fred was very impressed with me.

He was right, of course. Most gardeners just don't consider hiring contractors' plant for jobs in the garden, even for big jobs like changing levels or smoothing land for lawns or beds —they think it would be far too expensive. The trick is to get as much work as possible done for the £30 or so which it will cost to hire a Fred and his machine. If you do plan it all ahead, not only can you justify the hiring cost but also the cost, if necessary, of having a section of fence removed to allow access for the digger. Even if the access is too narrow for a tractor, there is usually a gap wide enough for a powerful motorized digger which can do the work of several men with spades and barrows.

However, I didn't have a fence to remove. I did consider trying to change Fred's opinion of me by claiming that this was the result of careful planning, but I didn't think he'd believe me.

The first job I got Fred to do was to create an earth barrier along part of the upper edge of the garden. He got through that so quickly that I'd had barely time to ask Doff to remind me about the other jobs, when he was back awaiting instructions.

There was the laurel crown to do, but I wanted to leave that till last—I was a bit wary of worrying Fred with such a minor problem. So we told him about the damp patches on our wallpaper. Soon after our arrival we'd realized that it was possible to trace the level of the soil outside the wall of the house by studying the line of damp patches on the mildewing wallpaper inside. As so frequently happens, the previous tenants had piled soil against the walls above the floor level in the old section of the house and even above the damp-course level at the Victorian end. We had dug away some of the soil but there was still plenty of work for Fred. Lowering the claws of his narrow inverted digger into the soil alongside the walls, Fred drew it back and smoothed it out with the ease of a cat scraping its litter. Later, by working the digger parallel to the stone wall, he also excavated a shallow ditch, 'to allow the foundations to breathe'.

We were worried that, after so many years of suffocation, the fresh air would be bad for them. But one should never doubt the wisdom of a Fred. Within days the walls dried out completely. The damp-proof material with which we were lining them became superfluous. And the shallow 'breather' trench was quickly hidden by a hedge of closely planted Munstead dwarf lavender, which we immediately established along its edge.

When he'd finished all the major jobs we felt his machine could accomplish, I nodded apologetically towards the laurel crown. I couldn't delay it any longer. Knowing the great division of labour in the country, however, I was very worried about how a contractor like Fred would react to being asked to involve himself in trivia like gardening.

It had taken me ages just to start the job of removing the fifty-year-old laurel which almost completely curtained the back of the house. I had finally freed the crown, and had then come up with the brilliant idea of replanting it. The only problem was that I would need a huge hole to put it in, and that it would take four strong men to move it. Or a digger.

'All right, then, where do you want it?' asked Fred, looking pained. I walked him round to the front of the house and pointed to a very draughty gap in the hedge. Driving like Niki Lauda, he roared the digger up to the spot and, with three quick bites, dug an immense hole.

I almost had to run as I followed him round to the back of the house to pick up the crown of the laurel. The machine did all the work. I simply had to steady the great woody lump as, looking like a bizarre sea creature, it was rushed round to the hole and lowered into place. I piled back the beautifully broken soil and the laurel found a new home.

I realize today that the trivial nature of the job might only have been partially responsible for Fred's impatience. Perhaps he was a secret gardener and knew that the operation was hardly worth the diesel fuel spent upon it.

The laurel has grown all right. Within a few weeks new shoots had begun to appear along all its exposed surfaces. But, even today, seven years later, they are barely four feet tall; so that wind from the south-west still cuts in to that corner of the garden. Had I planted four or five well-established new young laurels instead, they would have grown into a thick seven-foot-high screening hedge by now.

Still, at the time it seemed like a triumph of planning and

co-ordination. My sense of elation lasted as long as it took Fred to drive down to the road. At the top of the track I was basically a good planner who had been unlucky; by the time he got to the bottom I was a self-confessed failure nervously standing on one leg wondering whether I dared chase after Fred to tell him I had forgotten something.

I didn't. A weak-willed bad planner. Moving that giant mound of unearthed boulders from one margin of the garden to another was now a job for Hellish Holidays.

Unfortunately it had been their job before. I could just hear foreman Cox's voice: 'No, I'm sorry, you'll have to do better than that. This is the fourth time we have moved that heap of rocks in as many months. Why can't you make up your mind?'

Still, if I was a bad planner, at least I was a dab hand at man-management. I knew just what was needed in a situation like this. Bribery. There still wasn't an 'r' in the month so it would have to be three ribs of beef.

It was an old trick but it still seemed to work. The cost of covering up for my errors was, however, increasing all the time. Now that at least the bathroom worked and some bedrooms were in commission, many of them turned up for supper on Friday night and left totally exhausted just after dark on the Sunday.

The expenditure of so much effort turned faddy eaters into voracious gluttons. Together with the bills for the peat, fertilizer, plants and tools which their increasing efforts demanded, I wondered how long I would be able to go on feeding them. And Lyn, who ran the village shop, was worried about how long *she* could go on feeding them. She asked if we could ring before 5 pm on a Friday to warn her just how many of the fine crusty loaves which her brother baked we would need; otherwise she felt that one weekend the village might run out of bread. And that was just the food. There was a drink problem too. When initially encouraging the workers' brigade, I hadn't realized just what thirsty work gardening could be. At first a couple of glasses of reasonable claret per meal seemed to suffice. But by the time the first hectic autumn planting was over, that ration was only enough to get us through the soup.

So, as their capacity for drink grew, the quality dropped.

Litre bottles of French Table were quickly replaced by the stuff which makes Magyar husbands hurry home in the evening. The Spanish Burgundy only lasted a fortnight and was replaced by two litre flagons of coloured Arno water from Italy. Then Frascati, Orvieto, Soave, Chianti and Valpolicella were all given a try. I was becoming desperate, when an article in a colour magazine revealed that someone was even selling the banana mush pumped out of the bilge of ships fermented and dyed. The dye was said to be of vegetable origin and non poisonous. That would do, I thought, to fuel the efforts I needed to get the first year's plants established. But would it, I wondered, make them sluggish in the mornings? I had noticed that the cheaper the wine, the longer they lingered over coffee and the later they started. It made them irritable and inefficient too. Like a Roman farmer, I began to worry about their health. Sick slaves were useless. I remember an occasion when Faber dropped the end of a length of guttering he'd been holding because he swore that he couldn't understand what I was shouting at him, against the wind, through a mouth full of screws. Things like that hadn't happened when we were drinking claret.

Faber understood. Perceptive as ever, the slaves conferred secretly during the week.

On the following Friday, when Doff was still sceptically eyeing her two-page shopping list, and wondering if we'd ever be able to pay the supermarket bill, Faber struggled through the door and launched a case of good Burgundy on to the table.

Shortly afterwards, Cox arrived and casually flopped down a leg of lamb. By the time the last car drew up, there was scarcely an inch of free surface left in the kitchen.

For most of the weekend, slaves kept stumbling over a whole case of grapefruit which Meadows had fetched early from Covent Garden and placed in the middle of the floor. No one could confirm his claim that it did wonders for the virility, but several slaves pleaded for light work next morning claiming they had badly stubbed toes.

Smoking a last cigarette before bed that night, I felt strangely elated. The better quality wine might have induced a lighter mood than usual, but the elation was prompted by the realization that my workforce seemed willing to feed itself.

That, I felt, was a truly noble spirit of collaboration. Precious labour like this should not be wasted. The answer was to plan everything well in advance. Almost immediately I began thinking about the next day's jobs.

Chapter Five

The brick wall of the outhouse was superbly old and crumbly, so that making a hole for the wastepipe from the washing machine was easy. Each thump on the cold chisel with my four-pound hammer cut out a neat wedge of red clay like a portion of cheddar cheese.

Encouraged by my rapid progress, I hammered more and more vigorously making a terrific noise. I had paused to catch my breath, when I glanced through the kitchen window and saw Doff standing with her hands over her ears. She nodded and pointed behind me. Turning round I saw a stranger standing beside his car waiting patiently for me to finish my job. With my ears still ringing, I wondered who he could be. The Lord of the Manor perhaps? He still owned the right to shoot game over our freehold and had, out of curiosity, paid a visit earlier in the year and chatted to Doff through an unglazed window. That seemed unlikely; there was still little planted on our land attractive to hare, pheasant, partridge or deer.

But his general allure suggested a prosperous countryman. The weatherbeaten cheeks were the hallmark of a man who spent much time out of doors. His fine Prince of Wales check suit, brown suede shoes and tweedy trilby would have been equally appropriate for a man reading the lesson in Church or strolling round the paddock at a race meeting.

Since the kennels were only a couple of miles up our track and hounds passed our door early every morning during their exercise, I thought that he might have had something to do with the hunt. His bushy sideburns certainly gave him the slightly Edwardian look of several of the people we'd seen following hounds since cub hunting had begun.

The stranger disappeared behind a cloud of blue smoke as he lit his pipe and then, looking up, realized I had stopped hammering. Laughing, he wafted the smoke away with his free hand.

Even as he said 'Good morning' I could tell he wasn't a local. There was a hint of the soft roundness which overlays almost everyone's accent in the Vale, but behind it there was still a trace of Durham. As I replied he realized that I too was an émigré from the north-east. It provoked a beam of surprised recognition.

Foreigners (people born beyond the barriers formed by the Tweed, the Tees, the Pennines and the North Sea) are quite right to suspect that exiles from the north-east form a loose but secret 'Geordie' brotherhood reminiscent of the Mafia. I am not free to reveal the signs which passed between us, but a bond was formed. The only remaining doubt in my mind about this new blood brother was that I still wasn't sure exactly why he had come.

'You rang,' he offered in explanation.

The summer was now drawing to a close. Soon Hellish Holidays would only be organizing weekend trips. Even the camp *kommandant* and his wife would have to spend the week in London. There were, however, four urgent jobs to be done in the garden.

I needed a permanent location for all the herbaceous perennials which I had merely set in a trench earlier in the summer. After some showers, they were beginning to root properly in their temporary home and I wanted to plant them in a border without too much root disturbance.

Something had to be done about transforming the building site around the house so that, by the following spring, it would be recognizable as a garden: the land in front of the house had to be levelled and sown with grass. And we had to have a fence.

Finally, now that parts of the interior of the house were parquet-floored and carpeted, mud was becoming a problem. I wanted to create a paved courtyard outside the back door using the stones which we had removed from the floor of the house.

I had been worrying about when and how these jobs could be done when I noticed a card in the window of a tobacconist in the local village. It advertised the range of useful services provided by an independent contractor. I had rung him; and he had arrived.

After a few minutes' chat, it was clear that Terry Carroll was a wonderful find, and I felt it worth walking him over the whole property slowly so that he could understand what we were aiming at in that first stage of garden layout. With a piece of chalk on a paving-stone I drew a rough plan, explaining that the house lay about halfway down the hypotenuse of a right-angled triangle. The hypotenuse itself sat more or less on the north/south line of our entrance track. The track continued along the western side of our land which sloped gently upwards towards the north, rising approximately 15 feet over the 120 yards of the boundary.

The top half of the triangle above the house (the northern end of the garden) was to be a lawn, studded with ornamental trees and shrubs. Both its long sides were sheltered by wonderful mature hedges. Near the house, the western hedge began with a splendid mature English oak and ran on as a mixture of young elm, young ash and hawthorn with elm predominating. A cluster of two elms and two tall damsons acted as a twiggy candelabra at the bottom end of the eastern hedge. Halfway up, another English oak made an exciting high point, echoed by a pair of fairly tall elms near the top of the garden. Most of the eastern hedge between the trees was white-flowered hawthorn with an occasional blackthorn.

This area also had interesting possibilities because, when the boundary was straightened before our purchase, a sliver of land—about a tenth of an acre—varying from two to four yards wide was added to the garden beyond the eastern hedge.

The land to the south of the house was also divided into two areas. A rectangular patch was bounded by the track on the west, the barn on the east, the house to the north and our open boundary on the south. Another rectangle of similar dimensions was bounded by the barn on one side and the cattle-shed along our eastern boundary on the other. It was in the area immediately south of the house, overlooked by the dining- and drawing-rooms, that Terry's help was most needed.

That part of the garden had already had a fair amount of attention. Advised by an expert on agricultural weed problems, I had applied a brushwood killer in diesel oil to the brambles and a water-based spray of Aminotriazole to all the soft vegetation. They seemed to have worked pretty well despite the strong challenge, and despite the fact that I had not applied the weedkillers at the optimum time: in spring when everything is growing vigorously.

Then Martyn had brought along his Australian earth-cracking disc plough, mounted on a tractor. He was worried about what successive generations of cattle feet and cart-wheels would have done to the earth. 'You'll never make a garden on soil compacted like this. You've got to get down into the subsoil. Improve the drainage and let the air penetrate. Plants are just like people: they need food, air and water.' So, with the eighteen-inch discs cutting into the summer-baked earth, he turned the garden upside down.

Cutting and turning the soil also helped to finish off the weedkiller's work. And any nasty root pests which had survived suddenly found themselves blinking in the daylight, about to become a bird's lunch. 'Funny,' said Martyn, watching as the birds tidied up for us, 'according to the conservationists they should all be dead.'

Looking critically at the ploughed patch in front of the house, Terry groped down among the furrows with his hands in several places and paced about before stooping down to estimate the gradient from different angles. He always worked like this, making a slow and careful appraisal of every problem before suggesting a solution. It meant that the solution was usually the correct one.

'If we just smooth it over and rake it into a seed bed, the lawn will always be very steep,' he said finally, after smoking away nearly half the tobacco in his pipe. 'If you ever want to play croquet on it, it will be a nightmare. There's not enough topsoil at the top end to simply level it out by raking towards the bottom, so we'll have to dig some out from further up the garden,' he continued in reply to my questioning look. 'Don't worry, that won't be any bother,' he added, seeing the dejection which was beginning to show.

I was already regretting being hasty about sowing the lawn at the top end of the garden. I knew that there had been plenty of spare topsoil there that the slaves would have enjoyed barrowing to the bottom. I'd been a victim of my own poor planning again. Terry reassured me that he would find the soil at the foot of the hedge and at the very apex of the triangle of the garden, beyond the eastern hedge.

He agreed with me that the best place to create the first herbaceous border would be against the south-west facing wall at the top end of the barn. There it would receive the full benefit of the sun for much of the day, be protected from the cold north and east winds by the barn itself and be directly in the line of vision from the windows of the house in the rooms most frequently used. If we had to rely on a single herbaceous flowerbed—as we would during the next summer—then, apart from the suitability of the aspect, it would be as well to put it in the most visible place possible to encourage us.

Initially we pegged out a large semi-circle with the barn wall as the straight edge. But then, on reflection, we thought it would look more interesting if the shape was asymmetrical, so we moved the pegs. This allowed us to increase the distance from the outer edge of the bed to the wall at both its shallower ends. I was pleased about that because previous experience had taught us that shallow herbaceous beds are not very satisfactory. We had discovered on the Downs that you need a minimum bed-width of four feet if you are to provide sufficient variety of plants in terms of size, shape and colour, and to ensure that there will always be something in flower in the area at any time throughout the summer.

Happily, at its widest, the bed would be nearly ten feet deep leaving room to grow the really large subjects like hollyhocks and shrub mallows, which must be allowed plenty of space to develop properly and express their full grandeur.

Picking up a fork, which was resting against the barn wall, Terry probed the area of the proposed bed and winced. 'It's full of stone. We'll have to get a pick at that lot, and I think I'd better get it done before we level the lawn. We won't want to mess up the prepared surface with the junk we are sure to dig out of here.'

Moving to the area outside the back door he came to a much quicker decision. 'The last thing you want here is anything resembling an urban patio. Nothing fancy. I suggest a simple rectangular paved area, running from the outhouse at the back to the front of the house and reaching out to a yard short of that tree.' He grimaced at the badly scorched ash about fifteen feet from the house.

I was delighted by his immediate grasp of the simplicity we sought. I could envisage the outer edge of the paved area culminating in a low stone wall with a raised bed behind it. With the slaves I had already planted a line of Lonicera cuttings level with the tree and parallel to the house wall to form an enclosing hedge at that side of the proposed court.

While I was already imagining the snug feeling there would be in the court when the hedge had grown tall, Terry was estimating the area of paving we had available. 'We need a third as many again to complete the job,' he concluded. He guessed from my hesitation that the cost of beautiful stone slabs might be embarrassing. But once more he came to my rescue unasked.

'They don't need to be stone. You could use Cotswold-based cast-cement paving-slabs. If I turn them rough side up and mix them among the stone I think they'll blend quite happily. There'll still be enough stone showing for it to look solid, and grit worn off the stone will soon be walked on to the rough surface of the cement—that'll improve the match.'

It was good advice which anyone could follow to reduce the cost of paving and maintain the strong visual appeal of real stone.

We wandered on, up to the top 'lawn'.

Terry grinned. 'You do need a fence, don't you.'

The slaves had flattened the area after Martyn had been through with his Australian earth-cracker, and had cleared off the vegetation and small stones. Then we had sown a mixture of creeping red fescue and dwarf perennial rye grass: rugged but fine grasses which Chris Backhurst, a man who has created golf courses all over the world, had suggested could be easily established on reasonably fertile and well-drained soil raked smooth. It was theoretically the wrong time of year, since in midsummer there is thought to be insufficient soil moisture for germination, but we were lucky enough to have several thunder showers. (We have since discovered that the Vale is usually that 'lucky'.) Sadly rain does not just swell seed. It also softens the surface of the ground.

Terry and I gazed at the devastation. The whole surface of the embryo lawn—which at the time was just showing a flush of tiny hair-like green blades, called 'Mother Earth's pubics' by a witty slave—was pock-marked with three-inch deep hoof marks.

By now I was beginning to get the idea. Gerhart thought we needed a fence. Terry thought we needed a fence. So did George, the stockman on the neighbouring farm. He had frequently provided valuable information and advice while stopping to gossip, and had always ended up by urging us to fence our land. 'More private and much safer,' he had said.

Apart from the fact that I might need to get heavy machinery into the garden, I was still romantically toying with the agreeable notion that the garden should simply flow out into the landscape and that fences were unpoetic restrictions which affected the spirit adversely. Town gardeners might need fences to keep out young urban guerillas and aspiring Kevin Keegans—I had a deeper, more profound need. I tried to make George understand this view on several occasions but, while expressing a certain sympathy, he always ended up vehemently exhorting us to 'get the place fenced about'.

No one knew whose cattle had stampeded through our garden. They certainly weren't George's. He was far too good a stockman and too shrewd in his handling of a herd to allow that to happen. But I now appreciated that the drawback of having a garden which flowed out into the landscape, was that the cow's landscape, equally, tended to flow out into my garden.

I thought we needed a fence.

The overall effect of the cattle's visit was not unlike that of a typhoon. A large-leaved viburnum, which we had nursed through transplanting when several of its stems were already six feet high (and which we were relying upon for some white blossom and bright red berries), had had three stems ripped away from one side. It looked like a half-lit gas ring.

Two lower branches of an eight-foot laburnum which was just starting to develop an impressive mature shape hung limp at the end of the torn bark which still connected them to the trunk.

A newly planted fine Canada Balsam whip keeled drunkenly away from its stake.

The greengage which we hoped would become a pretty and productive feature near the apex of the garden, now had its crown touching the ground and resembled one of the more bizarre Tasmanian indigenous tree ferns. Mercifully, when bowled over, its roots had been drawn out of the still loose planting soil as cleanly as healthy teeth.

Surveying the desolation, Terry tutted in sympathy but continued to grin. 'If you don't mind, I'll leave tidying up this lot to you. I'll get on with the fence.'

Chapter Six

Before I met Terry, I had believed that the basic tools for gardening were a spade and a stout fork. That was a delusion which he quickly dispelled.

I drove back up the track early one morning, a few days after Terry had first come round, having popped down to the garage to get the battery topped up and to ooze charm at their mechanics. (For vital maintenance on some of the more elaborate gardening tools, it pays to cultivate the local garage.) I thought I recognized Terry's car at the top of the track, but when I walked round the end of the house he didn't seem to be about. Peering down the garden against the low morning sun I saw a man I didn't recognize working near the barn. I assumed that he was one of Terry's men. As I approached I was immediately impressed by the width of his old trousers; relics of a bygone era, they were almost as broad as Oxford bags and would have suited W. C. Fields very well. The man was bending over a pick plunged deeply into the ground trying to obtain leverage on a buried rock. But even in that position, the trousers were so full that what had once been expensive tweed hung in loose folds like an elephant's behind.

I coughed to make my presence known, extraordinary things happened to the trousers. I tried to suppress a giggle. As the figure straightened up, I discovered that it was not one of Terry's men inside them; it was Terry.

He could only have been working for about twenty minutes and already two sizeable piles of large rocks and miscellaneous plant root had begun to accumulate just outside the line of pegs which marked out the future herbaceous bed.

'I told you we'd have to go down deep,' he said grinning as he nodded towards the excavated stones. 'Your roots wouldn't have had much chance of getting through that lot. It's hard enough for the pick and for the one we are on now we will need a crowbar.'

Terry's generosity is amazing. He showed no impatience with me for my initial reluctance to have the land prepared down to a full twelve inches. Heretical and impatient as ever (and worried about the expense), I had argued for a single-spit dig of six inches. He hadn't made much attempt to hide his disdain.

'Please yourself—you're paying. But I think you'll regret it. By next spring all the weeds which are lurking down there will have come up to strangle your plants and the only way to get them out will be to dig the whole lot up again.'

But there were no gloating 'I told you so's' now. He was even saying 'we' would need a crowbar—when he'd finished, the achievement would, I discovered, be 'ours'. Generosity is not, however, his only quality. It is just one of the exceptional qualities of an exceptional man.

During our first interview I had presumed that he managed a contractors business which employed squads of workers. However, he soon made it clear that he liked to do most of his client's work himself.

When he'd first left agriculture he'd managed teams of men for contractors laying airstrips and fencing miles of highway. Later, when founding his own business, he, too, had become an employer. He found it relatively easy to get the jobs which were too small to interest large contractors, but the obligation to provide continuous employment for his men became irksome, and so he decided only to seek work which he could tackle by himself and where he could be certain it would be accomplished to his own exacting standards. If he needed help with some of the heavier jobs, he had a group of self-employed craftsmen friends on whom he could call. By the time we met, this was a pattern of working into which he had comfortably settled.

As he grabbed for his crowbar and gradually worked it round and below the hidden rock, his thoroughness was apparent. The rock was clearly deeply buried—many gardeners would have been tempted to leave it hidden—but he knew that a stone left within spade reach would always present problems and was determined to disinter it.

Watching, I appreciated how little real effort was needed to accomplish such a heavy task with the right tools. Once he was sure that he'd got the point of the bar below the bottom of the rock—by gently thrusting it into the ground and allowing its weight to do most of the work—he pulled down the top end like a lever and made the rock explode through the soil surface.

When we'd dragged the rock off the bed area and gone back to inspect its yawning crater, I realized that while removing it Terry had done a fine job in breaking up the soil for inches all round. In retrospect, that, too, is the great advantage of using a pick and crowbar when first digging over an area of land. Apart from getting rid of the rocks it accomplishes more than half of the vital cultivations. When Terry had finally worked over the whole plot with his pick or bar to remove the large stones and large plant trash, he could very easily use his spade and fork to complete the preparation.

When I started transplanting all the perennials into the new bed, I was even more impressed with the thoroughness of Terry's work. Each time I plunged my long-handled trowel into the ground, the loose soil—each square yard mixed with a barrow-load of finely broken-down, well-rotted manure from the cattle-shed—seemed bottomless. In digging more than fifty holes I had found no trace of the roots of the thistles, docks or couch grass which had previously infested the site.

Of course Terry had been right. You can skimp a lot of jobs in the garden if time is short but it never pays to cut the effort when making new beds on virgin land. Deep digging, apart from enabling weeds to be removed, improves drainage and the aeration of the roots. It also allows large quantities of well-rotted organic matter to be mixed with the mineral soil ingredients at all levels. This greatly improves the retention of moisture which can save plants in times of drought. It isn't necessary to have a cattle-shed full of animal manure or to make compost: a whole lorry-load of wonderful sweet-smelling hops from a brewery or spent mushroom compost can be obtained in most places for less than £10. And the incorporation of the hops into the soil on a warm day can be satisfying inebriating work.

As I dug some holes for the pot-grown primulas, I continued to think about Terry. Here, I realized, was a genuine rural renaissance man. There didn't seem to be anything which he couldn't do well and quickly and now, outside the edge of the bed I was planting, there were mounds of rock and small stone which would keep the slaves barrowing and out of mischief for hours.

We had needed a low stone wall to mount a window frame to create a new porch on the site of the old one. Terry had built it superbly in a day. Glancing to my right, I looked again at the attractive rough oak fence between the barn and the track. No more horseboxes or Beastly-Trouts.

Apart from a few critical heartwood fence-posts, Terry had saved me a fortune in timber by constructing the whole fence out of off-cuts. He sensibly pointed out that I didn't need the expensive wood which I would have bought, since my aim was to plant an impenetrable hedge along the fence. Once the hedge was established it wouldn't matter if the fence gradually rotted away. 'Meanwhile,' he said, confirming his good taste, 'I think that rough-cut wood looks much more natural.'

As I worked I could hear the regular thud of a well-slung sledge-hammer as Terry, at the top of the garden, drove home the posts along which he'd stretch the wire designed to keep phantom cattle from entering the garden along our north-eastern boundary. Each time the head of Terry's hammer struck the top of a post, the noise it made ricochetted from the trees. The sound of every stroke seemed to be repeated. With my head down working I'd got used to the double sound he made.

Having scooped out five holes large enough to take the pot-bound roots of the primulas comfortably, I had filled them with water. There was no need to worry about manure in these holes because Terry had mixed it with all the soil in the bed.

When the first hole had drained sufficiently, I stooped to plant the first primula. Terry began driving in another post. Before I'd finished scraping back the soil and firming it about the roots I became aware of a third and closer noise. At first,

I thought it must be another ricochet caused by Terry working from a different angle. But this third lapping sound continued when Terry had obviously stopped hammering.

The noise seemed to be coming from behind my watering-can, which was alongside the first hole. Standing up, I looked behind the watering-can and was amazed to see a small animal calmly wiping its mouth with a lick of its long pink tongue. Aware of my presence, the creature looked back up at me with dark and mournful eyes.

It looked very like a red horizontal version of Jimmy Savile. Although no expert in zoology, I couldn't believe that the South Midlands harboured any such large mammal which I hadn't heard about. Too small to be a fox, its legs were far too short even for a cub. And, in any case, its lack of fear in my presence and the maturity of its gaze told me immediately that it was adult. I had once edited a book about dogs but, since the illustrations had been added later by the publishers, I was no expert in dog recognition. However, when it whoofed and wagged a plumey tail I was bound to conclude that it was indeed a dog.

Realizing that I was harmless and probably not worth bothering about, it once more dipped its long Savile snout into the remains of the muddy water and began lapping again.

Suddenly aware of what was happening, I lunged forward and tried to shoo it away.

Terry had rightly suggested that land which had been rained on for so many years would be almost bound to have turned rather acid and need some sweetening lime. 'And,' he said, 'land that's been under grass is always crawling with pests, so that no matter how many the birds have gobbled, we'd better put on some soil insecticide as well.'

Although the chlordane we had chosen was said to be barely poisonous, I didn't feel that I was prepared to connive at Jimmy Savile's death.

He accepted my rebuke good-naturedly, watched with some alertness as I planted the rest of the primulas and then chummily escorted me back to the house to fill the can for the final watering. Although I strolled slowly he had such short legs that he had to run. As the tiny pads beat like pistons at the ground his copious hair spilled in all directions and even my hard heart began to warm to him.

He waited deferentially outside when I went into the kitchen to fill the can and when I came out he seemed absorbed in what I took to be the exciting scent of a rabbit. Ignoring my hospitable, 'Come on then', he continued to sniff about the base of the ash tree as I went off down the garden.

Before I reached the primulas, there was a slight rustling of long grass as Jimmy leapt through the fence at the bottom of the garden and ran towards me. Certain that he couldn't have passed me, I wondered how he could have possibly run round the house, down the track into the field and come back through the fence more than a hundred yards in the time it had taken me to cover twenty-five paces.

I was even more disturbed when he came through the fence again a few seconds later. And again. And again.

Looking back towards the house, I could still see Jimmy sniffing round the ash tree. But beyond him there were four more Jimmys chasing each other in circles on the upper lawn.

By the time I looked back at least three more had started to collect about my legs.

Within half a minute they were pouring into the garden from all sides—round the corner of the house from the track, through the hedge beyond which Terry was working, across the flattened hardcore of the future tennis court. At a rough count there were nearly twenty, but they moved about so much that there seemed to be more.

Hot and confused from hammering, Terry crashed through the hedge and shouted, 'I think we are being invaded.'

His cry obviously had some hidden significance because simultaneously all the Jimmy Saviles began to bay. So many canine voices produced a fluting cacophony evocative of a medieval hunt in woodland.

Soon the chorus was joined by a throatier baritone bark as a much larger and more corpulent, floppy-lugged, Irish Water spaniel bounded on to the scene like Rudolph Nureyev wrapped in a curly brown carpet. His spectacular arrival stimulated the Jimmy Saviles to even more hysterical choruses. Above the pandemonium, I just heard Terry whoop, too, as he seemed to be joining in the melee. Three of the Jimmy Saviles had dragged his jacket from behind the hedge and were starting to pull it down the lawn. Lunging to snatch it back he tripped over the bulkier Water spaniel and tumbled on to one knee. As the spaniel yelped, the Saviles made off with the jacket now baying in triumph.

The din was building to a crescendo more noble than the high point in the overture to Tannhäuser when it stopped as abruptly as it had begun. An instant later, the invisible maestro stepped from behind the house.

I hadn't heard his command over the noise of barking but I learned later that the dogs could detect it and would obey instantly, even when Concorde was thundering overhead.

A stocky, rather handsome man in early middle age, he looked as though in his time he might have been a fine scrum half. As the dogs obediently collected in a pack about his heels, he smiled his good morning and apologized for their noise.

'They always seem to become very excited round here,' he explained. 'Last time they were down they put up a rabbit near your shed and I suspect that there must be something still about.'

Since we were now beginning to plant seriously, and many of our plants had been ruined on the Downs when myxomatosis had lost its potency, I was very interested in the rabbiting potential of his dogs. They were, he explained, members of one of the few full packs of purebred Long-Haired dachshunds in Britain, gentle and friendly for the most but quite fearless and ruthless when hunting. In their native Bavaria, they are used for hunting badger and wild boar.

I welcomed his promise that whenever he passed he'd let the pack scurry through the garden. And I'm sure now that without their menace, the rabbits would have destroyed even more plants.

Few new gardeners could be lucky enough to have a pack of hounds on call I thought happily as Terry and I watched its owner, with a brisk command, usher the dogs across the track, through a stile and away over the meadow. When he let them have their heads, they splayed out in front of him, barking and tumbling. Even quite small tussocks of grass became, for them, serious obstacles over which they had to bounce. Surging forward, they moved over the pastures like bounding red waves. Not for them the arrow-like directness of foxhounds on a scent; their progress was as unruly as their auburn locks.

I turned to Terry as he moved down the lawn to retrieve his crumpled jacket. He leaned forward to pick it up. We both started. A sleeve began to jerk convulsively and, as we watched, a tiny rabbit—it couldn't have been more than eight inches long—emerged through the cuff, paused for a second and dashed for the cover of the tangled ivy at the bottom of the hedge. Both of us were too amazed to react quickly. By the time we reached the hedge, nothing stirred despite our threatening cries and we were forced to call off the hunt.

'Did you ever,' exclaimed Terry, astonished by such audacity. 'They'd have had it if he hadn't called them off.'

'What discipline,' I reflected aloud.

'That's as may be. But you'll regret it because when you have got one of those little devils you can be sure that you have got a lot.'

Dashing back into the kitchen to tell Doff about the whole adventure, I was received very sourly. Refusing to listen, she simply pointed to the water splashed about the sink and the muddy gumboot marks on the newly laid parquet floor.

I knew she was right. I promised that I would buy the basic piece of equipment every gardener's wife knows that every gardener needs: an outdoor tap, with a threaded outlet for the hose. And I'd get a crowbar while I was about it.

Chapter Seven

'Mm,' murmured Mike, smiling knowingly. 'You obviously haven't discovered army field telephone wire. You're not reading your *Exchange & Mart* carefully enough.'

At first he'd been annoyed by my visit. Checking his order for the hundreds of varieties of shrub he needed for the autumn container planting programme was an important and trying aspect of his work. It required absolute attention.

'My God,' he'd said, sounding pained. 'Hasn't your holiday finished yet?'

His desk looked like the aftermath of an artillery bombardment. But Mike can never resist the challenge of a gardening problem and he was soon involved in helping me with mine.

After a morning leaning out from the top of a ladder, hanging on to the bricks with my fingernails, I was fed up. Having hammered lots of thick masonry nails into the wall, I'd been trying to stretch wire between them to support the new growth of the climbers I had planted early in the summer. The chilly breeze numbed my normally agile fingers and its sudden gusts made the operation even more dangerous. But the main cause of my anger was the wire I'd bought from a specialist gardening shop in London.

'I want something very tough which will last for years,' I'd explained.

'Ah well, this is expensive, but it's what you require,' the knowing assistant confidently assured me, proffering a very workman-like looking, stiff carton reel, with yards of fine wire clad in acceptably discreet, dull green plastic coating.

'The plastic prevents corrosion,' he continued, flipping a length he'd drawn from the reel expertly with his fingers.

Since I was reluctant to festoon the house with either wood or plastic trellising, strong thin wire seemed the best alternative. So, innocently, I paid the exorbitant price.

Sadly, I discovered, hovering on the ladder, that the wire was a dreadful swizz. Each time I tried to pull it taut, it snapped with a chilling whine. I had visions of losing an eye as the released end whipped past my cheek.

'Now this stuff,' said Mike, plunging his fingers into the dusty scramble of brown-coated wire on the floor and raising the strands like a man about to eat spaghetti, 'this stuff is strong enough to hang from.'

We were in the glory hole of the nursery. A fine stone-built hall, large enough to stage a gracious ball, it was packed with a horticultural miscellany. Clearly there was once order here, but time and impatience had brought about a catastrophic dishevelment.

The rolls of rabbit wire, stacks of fence-posts, wooden gates, drums of chemicals and bags of special fertilizer were fairly neatly arranged, but any sense of order was upset by the presence of other, wholly inappropriate objects.

A fine directory chaise longue with striped silk upholstery and a group of Sheraton chairs—evidence that Martyn and Imogen had once more embarked upon a doing-up campaign—added a strange note of elegance. Sixteen splendid twelve-foot-high cast-iron Doric columns which had once held aloft the balcony of a Methodist Chapel in Wales loomed with dignity and provided a wonderful barrier to circulation.

It was very difficult to spot the origin of the wire which Mike held aloft. It was even more difficult, as we found a minute or two later, to discover a free end.

There seems little doubt that, no matter how ill-prepared we were for the Hitler war, the army was determined to see that we should not run short of wire. Perhaps, as someone suggested, the War Office planned to issue all troops with lengths of wire so that the enemy could be tripped and garrotted to defeat. Whatever the reason, they got in enough wire not just to last out the war, but the following thirty-four years as well. There still seems to be plenty of the stuff left. For this, generations of civilian gardeners can be grateful, because it is the best possible material for tying up roses and climbing plants.

However, like many items of ex-W.D. stock, it comes in bewildering quantities. Even today it is advertised in *Exchange & Mart* at only £12 per third of a mile. Such a length of wire stores, quite tidily, on a reel. Unfortunately it is totally unmanageable when released.

Martyn's Weimarana, Pad, had found such a lengthy snake irresistible. Creeping into the hall unnoticed, the dog had grabbed the free end of the wire between his teeth and dragged about a quarter of a mile of it all over the hall. There wasn't a fence-post, chair leg, roll of netting or column base which wasn't locked into the resulting web. Glancing over the tangle, Mike looked apologetic. 'If you want it now we'll simply have to find an end and get unweaving.' It took nearly an hour of patient unravelling to provide me with an adequate coil to support most of my climbers.

Looking at the early growth, it was clear that supporting the plants correctly would be trickier than I thought. Several fairly vertical strands of wire running from a point near the root to nails high up on the wall would, I believed, hold the rapidly growing leading stems of the honeysuckle and clematis. It was already obvious that their hundreds of lateral stems would join hands in mid air and, once entwined, support themselves—very few horizontal wires would be necessary. I did create two for the clematis, to be able to lead it at a medium and high level from the front round to the eastern side of the house. Although it was growing less vigorously, while I still had the ladder out, I also made a lateral leadway to take the honeysuckle across the top of the drawing-room window.

But roses, I knew, were different. Alex Cocker, the breeder of Alex's Red, Silver Jubilee and many other famous roses, had told me that if I wanted climbing roses to flower best I must keep trying to bend their main stems back towards the ground. I found that, to follow his advice, many more horizontal wires were necessary. Instead of a surge for the sky, it was clear that with roses the ascent would have to be accomplished in a series of looping steps.

It was late afternoon by the time that I had finished stringing and tying. Up the ladder I'd been aware that I was not the only person busy in the district. The main harvesting of winter wheat was underway in the fields around. Tractors with brimming trailer loads of grain had been trundling down the track past the house as frequently as lorries down the M1. From time to time, I'd been aware of the noise of a smoother engine and looked down to see Farmer Green's Marina speeding by in front of a cloud of dust.

I was amazed by what the sturdy suspension of this smart saloon could take. Farmer Green's son, Robert, was using the Land Rover and the pace of work on the farm was too urgent to allow time for walking, so the saloon had to double as a work vehicle for the day. While I always drove down the track gingerly, like a maiden aunt taking an outing in a landau, Farmer Green tackled it like James Hunt completing the last victorious lap of a Grand Prix.

Not that his racing talents were confined to the track. A forthright and direct man, he firmly believed that the shortest distance between two points was a straight line. So, if the field he was heading for was on the other side of a cow pasture or a patch of already harvested land, he would beat his own highway across it. An aerial photograph of the farm at the time would have looked something like Spaghetti Junction, with our house locked in its middle.

There was something unnerving about the sight of a Marina doing forty amongst cows placidly grazing emerald grass. But when Farmer Green was busy, it became quite commonplace.

I had just brought down the ladder when he sped up the track again with even more frightening urgency. I ran round to the back of the house to have the pleasure of watching him fly past. Instead of this, the car squealed to a halt and Farmer Green leapt out.

At first I thought he looked very ill. His cheeks and the brow beneath the peak of his cap were clearly healthy enough—underneath a thick covering of brown dust the skin glowed pink from exertion and the days of exposure to wind and sun—but his eyes, while still twinkling, were set in two large and disturbing pale oval patches.

Aware of my anxiety, he laughed. 'Don't worry about that. It's only my goggles.' He didn't need the ton-up-boy goggles slung around his neck for quick laps of the cow pasture, but he did need them on the combine harvester. Tiny, infuriatingly gritty fragments of the chaff and awn of the grain always fill the turbulent air around the machine: 'Without something to protect our eyes we'd go blind.'

Looking past him I realized that the Marina was almost new. I could still see bits of the protective polythene covering hanging off the seats.

'You're giving it a good old test,' I commented.

'Ah, she's not bad,' he replied with conviction. 'Barely run in yet.'

'Will she stand the rough work, do you think?' I asked.

'Suspect she might. Better had. Still under guarantee, you know.'

While I was reflecting on this personal challenge to the Marina's designer, Farmer Green, who normally said exactly what he thought, looked vaguely embarrassed.

'Wondered if you'd mind obliging,' he said tentatively.

I couldn't think what I could do to help him. In the six months since we'd bought the house I'd been obliged to call on him or his son (our immediate neighbour to the west) for many favours. We had been provided, in a great spirit of generous neighbourliness, with all manner of things: heavy timber to shore up the wall of the barn; tractors to tug careless slaves and their Citroens out of ditches; a mower to cut down the weeds; advice on everything from the best place to put the overflow pipe of the septic tank to the local specialist shops. On one occasion when we were away, Robert had noticed that some jackdaws, on the look-out for a nesting site, were admiring our newly swept chimneys—so he brought his ladders round and fixed metal grids to the chimney tops. Apart from having depressed them with an early prediction of the increase in cattle-food prices, I had not been able to render them any services in return for their kindness.

''Fraid we've been a bit slow in widening the entrance of that gate,' Farmer Green said apologetically. Terry's new fence between the bottom of the barn and the track had the effect of narrowing the gateway into the field beyond.

'Forgot all about it until five minutes ago,' Farmer Green explained. 'We always used to take the machines in through here,' he continued, indicating a path from the back of the house across the foundation for the tennis court and out into the field between the barn and the cattle-shed.

'That's fine,' I said, rather hesitantly, looking at the line of new posts Terry had just finished installing for a fence—just where the combine harvester would cross from the garden into the field.

He reassured me. 'Don't you worry about them. We only need to have two out and we'll have them back in no time. It was when I was passing earlier and saw them going up that I realized we were being locked out.'

The small section of established lawn which his machines would have to cross seemed dry enough to allow tractors to pass without damage. And manufacturers had assured me that combine harvesters exerted no more pressure per square inch on the ground than a man. The fat tyres on the trailers, should, theoretically, spread the loads of corn equally well; so with what I hoped was good grace I told him he was welcome to use his traditional route.

With autumn approaching, and our timetable for having the house habitable and the garden established getting tighter all the time, the prospect of actually having to undo some work on the fencing was upsetting. We'd already had enough problems with Gerhart and his wretched swallows.

While the window frames were removed from one of the main bedrooms for repair, a swallow family had seized its chance and built a nest in a corner of the ceiling. We discovered it on the morning the window was to be replaced.

Gazing up at it delightedly, Gerhart almost cooed. 'How lucky. It's a true blessing on this house.' He continued to wonder as I lost interest and began to move a repaired frame towards the window.

'Keep back,' he cried, gesturing towards me impatiently. 'Look, the mother, she's coming.'

As I stood aside, the swallow side-slipped through the window and with a few swift beats of the wings reached and settled over her nest.

Gerhart was thrilled, raising his forefinger in front of pursed lips he motioned me to be silent. After a further few moments of entranced gazing, he beckoned me to follow him out of the room through the door and closed it behind us, beaming.

'But the window,' I expostulated.

He laughed very knowingly. 'Ah well, there is no question

of that now. You will have to wait until she and her young are gone.'

'Can't we just move the nest and then get on,' I demanded impatiently.

'What—ruin your luck for ever and destroy that miracle of nature,' he asked astonished.

I could tell from his expression that he thought I was an unfeeling monster.

Then he relaxed and broke into his habitual smile. I must, he realized, have been joking.

'Hah!' he laughed, running off downstairs leaving me feeling frustrated and guilty.

A wise man knows when he is beaten and reluctantly I followed him down. When I reached the back door and stepped into the porch, which we were just about to enclose with plate-glass, Gerhart looked unnaturally bright. His features were oddly contorted and his eyes shone like a man who has seen a beautiful vision. In this experience of Nirvana his cheeks, too, had heightened in colour. I wondered whether he was going mad.

Afraid of upsetting him, I smiled gently and said, 'What?'

'Look at that,' he crooned, pointing to the inside of the roof directly above my head.

As I followed his gaze, I received the first of several christenings on the shoulder from another swallow settling on to another newly made nest.

'Oh Hell,' I groaned, realizing that the porch, too, would have to remain open until the young had flown. 'This isn't a house, it's a bloody wildlife park.'

Gerhart nodded enthusiastically. 'What wonderful luck,' he shouted at me again when I went off down the garden feeling very disgruntled.

He was much less cheerful when, several days later, he led me upstairs and pointed to the bedroom floor. All I could see was what appeared to be two slightly fluffy stains on the boards. Bending down I realized that they were the forlorn remains of two baby swallows.

'They must have fallen out when the mother was away,' he said in a flat voice. He was very sad.

Over the days, while working outside in the garden, I'd become reconciled to the loss of glazing time and had even begun to share his enthusiasm for our guests. The agility with which the adults seemed to pause in flight and then plunge through the window carrying titbits to pop into the upturned beaks we'd glimpsed in the nest was delightful. When they were most active, just watching their antics absorbed almost more time than picking and digging.

So, when peering at the corpses and lamenting so much lost promise, I too was momentarily saddened.

'Pull yourself together,' my rational conscience told me. 'Nature is far too baffling for mortals to comprehend.'

'Ah well,' I said, standing up and trying to feel light-hearted, 'at least we'll be able to get on with the windows.'

I don't think I sounded very convincing, because neither Gerhart nor Doff who had joined us to share the tragedy seemed at all mollified.

'Bloody shame,' Gerhart muttered half to himself. Then, realizing the full implication of what had happened, he thundered: 'A terrible omen. Your house will never bear fruit and your garden will never grow.'

Glancing out at our highly attractive daughter, Liesi, who was sunbathing in front of the house. I thought at first, 'That at least is a blessing.' But when I saw the rose I'd planted against the barn wall, I allowed myself a doubt. When reason prevailed I became slightly irritated. I had had more than enough of Gerhart's Gothic mythology.

'Ah, come on. You don't believe all that stuff . . .'

My words died as his expression suddenly changed. Spreading his arms wide, he bustled both Doff and me out through the door. He bolted away from us down the stairs, and, totally mystified, we ran after him out through the back door and round to the front of the house.

'Look!' he cried. 'They are going to try again.'

As we watched, a swallow ducked out of the window, plummeted a few feet and then winged its way to join its mate, rocking gently on the electricity cable which led from the village to our house.

Liesi, a reluctant slave but enthusiastic topless sunbather, was disturbed by our sudden arrival. Hastily struggling into her bikini top, she joined us in peering up at the swallows.

'Isn't that great,' she declared, rather callously I thought.

'Yes, it's great,' Gerhart echoed. 'It means that everything is going to be all right,' and he ran off towards his beloved barrow.

'Marvellous,' Doff endorsed, which I felt was a bit disloyal.

'Well, suppose it is quite nice to have visitors from North Africa about the garden,' I managed to struggle out—not wanting my frustration at having to defer the glazing once again to be too apparent.

Thankfully the fledglings in the porch fared better; they soon out-grew their nest, learned to fly, and found themselves a more convenient roosting place in the cattle-shed.

The second brood in the bedroom also thrived and one morning Gerhart, who had forbidden us entry to the maternity ward, beamed happily as he took us up to point out the vacant nest.

Climbing on a chair, he gently detached it from the ceiling and almost covetously pointed out how wonderfully it had been constructed, using the sculptors' modelling technique of taking small balls of moistened clay and gently flattening them into place. Handing it to Liesi for closer examination, he said enviously, 'I wish to goodness I could build as well as that.'

Chapter Eight

Nothing transforms a landscape more rapidly than a combine harvester.

We had known the crop in front of our house since its youth. It had always been part of our landscape. When we had arrived the wheat was just waking up after its winter chilling—there was more soil visible than bright green spear. We'd seen the rush of foliage in response to the spring dressing of fertilizer, and then Robert's efforts to stave off rust disease and greenfly with sprays.

Later he had good-humouredly tolerated our amusement at his battles with the birds. He put up a scarecrow. The birds used it as a staging post, almost contemptuously besmirching the smooth felt of its bowler hat with excreta. He drove up and down the track, like a desperado in a gun battle, letting off his shotgun through the Land Rover window. Doff reckoned he would need another £2 per ton for his corn to pay for the cartridges. When the cartridges had run out, he resorted to constant hooting on the Land Rover's horn. But the strain on the battery was so great that eventually the 'hoot' sounded more like the wheeze of a dying asthmatic.

So he shouted and waved his arms. After one extraordinarily violent outburst—of which any Glasgow Rangers fan would have been proud—he noticed us watching with amazement.

'I spent two years at agricultural college,' he shouted. 'They taught me that crop protection is a scientific business.'

But, happily, all Robert's efforts that year were rewarded. And as Farmer Green brought the combine harvester up the track—with its grumbling engine and lurching gait it seemed like some great prehistoric beast forced to graze hostile terrain—I could not help but feel some of a farmer's excitement at the moment of harvest.

After his father's second tour of the headland, Robert checked the grain, taking a handful out of the harvester, rubbing it on his palm and raising it to his nose. Farmer Green lowered his goggles and turned round anxiously. Seeing Robert's grin and the raised thumb, he smiled cherubically, raised his goggles and let in the clutch. Robert had to leap off the machine as his father lurched round the corner of the cattle-shed for the third time.

Then the transformation began in earnest. The comforting barrier of the mature crop began to disappear. The combine harvester swept past, and the land was laid bare, soil visible again below a fakir's mattress of stubble.

This development was very unpopular with the rabbits. Obviously they had got up early on this fine morning and had gone out into the field to pick at the weeds between the wheat rows. Frightened by the harvester circling the field outside them, they had discreetly moved away from the noise towards the middle of the crop. But, as the band of corn which remained to be cut dwindled, more and more of them broke cover and bolted for the headland.

Watching their urgent flight was a recurring distraction from the task which I had chosen to fill the day.

Before leaving the previous garden, I had dug up an old matted clump of established pinks. On their arrival in the Vale they had been heeled into a patch of bare mud and left to fend for themselves. Vigorous plants, which seemed to enjoy abuse, they had thrived splendidly. But if we wanted fine thick pillows of pinks in our second summer I knew that I should get on with my work of splitting the plants.

Teasing apart the old intertwined stems, I had rejected all those which were too thick and brown looking and was able to break off taut young shoots with portions of root attached.

By the time the rabbits began to bolt, several square yards of garden path seemed to be covered with fragile-looking fragments. If they were to survive in such hot weather they needed planting and watering immediately.

Stooping to push them into a one-and-a-half inch layer of

fine gravel spread on the surface of Terry's bed was hard work in the sun. Pushing them into the gravel, which was necessary for good drainage, was easy. It was all the bending and stretching which made me sweat. Happily, Farmer Green's men provided me with relief.

Hearing the shouts of the tractor drivers used to ferry the grain to the farmstead, I abandoned gardening and wandered out to watch them chasing rabbits with sticks. The movement of the men was hampered by the windrows of cut straw which striped the ground. The rabbits either bounded over the mounds or, using them as cover, soon outran their pursuers.

We all heard the anguished squeal as the combine harvester began to cut its penultimate swathe. Frozen in terror a rabbit had crouched down until the machine was nearly upon it. Trying too late to leap clear, one of its legs had been severed as cleanly as the straw by the vicious cutter knives.

Obviously in agony, the animal's urge to survive overcame its initial shock. As the severed leg began kicking convulsively, the rabbit scrambled off to follow its fellows across the field. Swerving giddily, it managed to reach the hedge and disappear into a thicket of brambles before we arrived. Its track was flecked with the still brilliant scarlet of the blood which had pumped from the stump as it ran.

George tried unsuccessfully to find it and put it out of its misery. He failed. He did, however, discover the mouth of a warren and he suggested that the rabbits must all be hidden there. 'Suspect he'll die from loss of blood and shock,' George speculated, panting after his effort.

Having seen the rabbit's determination, I was doubtful, although it was going to be a poor sort of life for a rabbit who was missing one leg. Turning back to watch the last swathe being cut we were both astonished by the number of rabbits who had used it as a final refuge. As the band of corn began to disappear, more than a dozen of them scattered in all directions.

As I walked back across the field, I noticed something lying on the straw. I stooped to pick it up. It was the severed leg of the rabbit. A nasty talisman, I thought, hurling it away.

The homogenous, densely packed mass of the standing crop had now completely disappeared, and been replaced by the striped pattern of lines of windrowed straw which betrayed the path of the powerful machine. Several times after the harvester left the wheat field, when everything had lapsed into late afternoon tranquillity, I walked to the bottom of the garden to survey the change. I felt like a man who has had a long overdue haircut and can't resist peeping at himself furtively in the mirror every few minutes to re-examine the effect.

As I leant against the fence-posts I couldn't help worrying about the rabbits. I was seriously apprehensive about their effect on our garden. Their stealth, speed of movement and fanatical will to prosper would, I realized, make them a formidable enemy.

On my third trip down the garden to look at the field and worry about rabbits, I gazed at the hedge on the far side. And saw the fox again.

My father was the first to spot it, when he and my mother briefly visited the house soon after we bought it. They had been strolling slowly round the wilderness we had bought worrying, as parents will, about the wisdom of our investment.

'Martyn says it will be worth a fortune when it's done up,' I said.

Since they had met Martyn and Imogen, and been mesmerized by their charm, I felt that quoting Martyn as an authority would be reassuring. 'And that's the real reason for the purchase,' I continued, gesticulating towards the view across the Vale, trying to sound as convincing as Martyn had been.

They were following my gaze, still looking doubtful, when suddenly my father stiffened like a Pointer which had detected a scent.

'Hello,' he said excitedly. 'I think we are being watched.'

I couldn't see anyone.

Irritated, he prodded me in the shoulder and pointed across the young corn in the field beyond our boundary.

'Look, look, look—there—just below the hedge.'

As he spoke the fox which had been standing and staring in our direction turned and walked sedately away. We watched it entranced until, with a delicate hop, it sprang through a gap in the thick hawthorn hedge and disappeared.

'What a nerve,' I exclaimed.

'Ah, they know when they are in no danger,' Father stated

authoritatively. Both keen followers of a Northumbrian hunt, my parents were delighted. Any reservations they may have had about our investment vanished. Staying with us in future held the promise of good sport.

This time the fox was scurrying about. Walking slowly towards me into the field he would pause, raise his head as though sniffing the air, and then drop his nose to the ground. Apparently picking up an exciting scent, he would zig-zag for a few yards across and between the windrows. Stopping as abruptly as he had started, he looked confused, sniffed the ground all around him and then raised his head once more.

It took me some minutes before I realized he was trying to follow the dying scents of all the rabbits which had escaped from the combine harvester.

'Good luck, my boy, *bon appetit,*' I thought, happy to have an ally in the battle against the rabbits. I stubbed my cigarette out and returned to the kitchen to try and cadge some coffee.

I failed. Henriette, one of my best slaves, had donated a goose for supper and the kitchen was full of good smells and cooks. 'Out,' Henriette threatened, waving a fork menacingly in my direction when I muttered the word 'coffee'.

Even if it had been available I realized that I wouldn't have been able to stand drinking coffee in the kitchen.

I walked slowly back to look at the cut field again. As I rounded the corner of the barn and climbed up on to the tennis-court base I was astonished by my closest ever view of a fox. Only thirty yards away, near the other end of the court, he stood transfixed, with his nose stretched high in the air and his nostrils quivering.

Apparently hypnotized, he seemed quite unaware of my arrival. But his natural vigilance soon returned. An instant later all I could see clearly was his great brush pluming out behind him as he fled across the field.

I expected him to continue running until he had reached the haven of his lair somewhere in the far hedge. However, when he'd gone about 150 yards he slowed down, turned and halted. And then, with almost casual audacity, he craned his nose upwards and began to savour the air again. Realizing that I was still watching, he must have decided that I was a danger because, after some moments of sniffing, he relaxed, turned and walked back to his hedge.

Perhaps it was my imagination, but I thought by his drooping posture that he looked crestfallen. And as I turned back to the house I suddenly realized what had attracted him. The light wind had rounded to the north-west and, as it drifted past the house, it became impregnated with the wonderful aroma of good cooking.

The message was clear. To ensure that the fox continued to reside so close to the house that it could venture into the garden and scare away the rabbits, we would have to eat very well every day.

Of course, providing the daily attraction of goose would have led to bankruptcy. But from then on, whenever Doff stewed up the carcass of a chicken to make stock for soup, I insisted that she did it with both the door and the windows of the kitchen wide open. And it must have worked, because several times over the following two years—until the hedge, and with it the fox, disappeared—we saw him halfway across the field with his nose in the air. And during that period the rabbit problem was no more than a minor irritant.

Chapter Nine

The harvest was over; the combine harvester had left—the gateway had been widened to ensure Farmer Green access to his fields the following year. The surface of the tennis court was finished; the lorries and rollers used to put on the tarmac top had gone. Finally we could close all our boundaries permanently, not just with fence-posts and wire but with hedges.

First of all, though, I wanted to do some planting around the tennis court. A hard court is an ugly intrusion in a garden—an alien surface in an area which should be soft and natural. Even the foundations had been a bit of an eyesore, so I had been eager to plant out the sturdy young Cupressocyparis Leylandii trees which were to screen the court. Too eager, as usual.

Cox had learnt, from previous experience of my capabilities as a planner, to keep an eye on me. A few weeks before the contractors were due to arrive to tarmac the court, he watched me prepare to put in the Leylandii.

'And how are they going to get the machines on to the court without smashing the trees?' he asked rhetorically.

I had only chosen the Leylandii after much thought. They can look very sinister if allowed to grow to their full height—which, in graveyards, they often are. But no other really thick, evergreen, hedging plant grows so fast, which makes them ideal for gardeners as impatient as me. And, in a garden near Spalding in Lincolnshire, I had seen just how good they can look when grown as a close hedge, tightly clipped and restricted in height.

Cox helped me to plant the trees the day after the last machines had left. We placed them along two sides of a rectangle, to enclose all the top end of the court and run halfway down the west side. By planting them in two parallel lines, one yard apart, and setting them at one-yard intervals (with their placing staggered so that from a distance there only appeared to be half a yard between them) we hoped that they would soon produce an impenetrable mass of foliage.

Apart from acting as a visual screen between the court and the house, I thought that the hedge would make conditions less gusty on the court in windy weather. Since I also planned to use the protection offered by the hedge to shelter a small orchard in the future, we planted the northern arm seven yards away from the base line at the top of the court.

When, a few days later, Terry finished levelling the soil in front of the house and sowed the lawn, I was still trying to decide what to plant as a hedge along the southern boundary of the garden, between the barn and the track. I had to establish something that could eventually replace the rough wooden fence with its built-in obsolescence. A visit to Castle Howard in Yorkshire provided the answer.

Between the car park and the great house we passed ten-foot-tall billowing mounds of old shrub roses. Their tough, extremely thorny stems had become densely entwined and looked proof against even a charging bull. The vivid colours of their engagingly untidy clusters of blooms had a freshness which contrasted agreeably with the synthetic shades of many modern hybrid tea-roses. Best of all, they exuded a delicious fragrance.

When we brought the idea back to Mike Tucker he confirmed that, not only could we choose varieties which would flower at different times, but that there were varieties which, in favourable years, would bloom twice. 'Select five varieties, mix them all up and plant them at one-yard intervals—then you should have colour as well as foliage for most of the season. And in the autumn you'll have a magnificent show of differently shaped hips.'

I had doubts about mixing the colours of the roses indiscriminately. Patiently, Mike taught me one of gardening's fundamental lessons. 'Colours rarely clash in nature. You *can* make mistakes. But you won't very often. The character of natural pigments seems to ensure their harmony.' Even, as he pointed out, when flowers of two antagonistic colours are placed side by side. 'I suppose it's because each patch of violent colour is separated from the next by an area of subdued natural colour—soil, stems, or foliage.'

Since the boundary at the south end between the barn and the cattle-shed was largely hidden by the tennis court, the need for a hedge to go alongside Terry's strong wire fence was less urgent. And anyway we had an ever-growing cuttings bank which we could put there.

We had already discovered that gardeners, although prone to a jealousy of sufficient intensity to rupture life friendships, are innately generous people. When they hear that you have acquired a patch of virgin land they elect themselves midwives to its birth as a garden. Every time they dig up perennials in their own beds to thin and replant them, they set aside clumps of superfluous root for you. Each snippet of twig they prune from their shrubs, is taken with a corner of your garden in mind. They know exactly where they would plant it, 'if they were you'.

Although no new gardener could either dare or afford to reject this green-fingered charity, it can provide problems. The land may not be ready. Advice to 'just stick it in anywhere and it will grow like old Billy' is frequently difficult to follow.

Throughout the summer, before any work could be done, we had to dash round every corner of the garden watering fragments of plants which had been kindly donated and for which we had hastily had to find temporary homes in mounds of builders' rubble, trenches in the dung floor of the shed or even under upturned plastic buckets. The water in preserving jars in which cuttings were 'bound to put out a mass of roots in a few days' turned the filthy brown of cold tea and released an intolerable stench when knocked over.

As we discovered later, accepting such freely bestowed bounty also carries with it hidden problems. Deep in a knotted batch of iris corms or among the roots of a useful clump of asters can lie the infestive fragments of far more sinister plants. Nestled into a well-dug and fertilized bed with their carriers, they will sprout and prosper. And once established, these weeds are difficult to eliminate.

That's how we introduced the dreaded ground ivy into the

garden. In our haste to finish the first year's planting, we didn't vet the new arrivals carefully enough. Although we did spread sheets of plastic on the ground and try to tease out all the corms and roots, to be sure we planted only flowers and not the weeds, an inch or two of ground ivy root must have escaped our inspection. Unfortunately, an inch is all you need to start a garden full of the stuff: it has become our most persistent weed. And the second most persistent—the delicate, firtree like horsetails—arrived in the garden, we think, in amongst a pretty clump of golden rod.

Of course, when they discover that you too are plagued by *their* most problematical weed, the gardening philanthropists who have unwittingly bestowed it upon you are very pleased. 'Oh, you'll have a hell of a time with that one,' they say, beaming benignly. It is as though they feel that your friendship has been cemented by the arrival of a common enemy.

Happily that didn't happen with the Jerusalem artichokes.

'There's a fine carton of colic,' said the literary lady from north Oxfordshire as her husband dumped a cardboard box loaded with artichoke corms on to the bonnet of my car.

'But they do make delicious soup,' he protested in their defence. 'And they make a marvellously pretty lightning hedge.'

So we thought we would plant them in a line to form a temporary hedge at the bottom of the tennis court. Particularly after their donors had assured us that the artichokes would 'grow absolutely anywhere and never need attention'.

We planted the corms at fifteen-inch intervals about five inches deep in a dubious mixture of poor soil and fragments of the old railway ballast which had been used to make the base of the court. Despite this poor home, they grew well to provide a four-and-half-foot leafy screen topped by buttery petalled and black-eyed small sunflowers during the next summer.

Like all gardeners we were most concerned about our eastern boundary. That was the side from which the cold winds would blow.

At the top end of the garden, the eastern side was well screened by the established hedge. And beyond it, just inside the wire fence which Terry had put up, the Lonicera nitida cuttings which I had planted early seemed to have taken well after only being pushed down five inches into well-dug moist soil. The fact that Martyn had been careful not to handle the cut ends, when he had snipped the twelve-inch tips off an established hedge, and the fact that I had planted them within an hour of their being cut, had probably helped. When they grew tall they would, I hoped, provide a thick, evergreen, secondary line of defence. I would then, I thought, be able to remove some of the hawthorns from the existing hedge to make channels for vision, and allow the additional sliver of land beyond the hedge (which we had christened 'Poet's Walk' because of its seclusion) to become a more integral part of the garden.

Between the bottom of the hedge and the cattle-shed the eastern boundary was unscreened. Fortunately, a majestic line of thirty elms, beginning with the pair opposite our back door, ran out from our boundary towards the east. This would, we realized, act as a fine barrier against winds from the north-east.

Apart from a few stunted suckers from the elms, which were attempting to survive cattle constantly browsing over the barbed wire, nothing else of much value was growing on that margin when we arrived.

Happily, here too the Lonicera cuttings along the wire seemed to have taken, despite a struggle with tall grass and nettles. And, I was pleased to see, my young elderberry seedlings had shot up well.

Several gardeners had chastised me for, before leaving the Downs, I'd dug up several sturdy young seedlings and replanted them beside the elm suckers. 'You can't do that,' the orthodox had said. 'Nothing will ever grow in your garden again.'

Having already done it several times before, I knew that they were wrong.

The fact that the elderberry grows so vigorously and spreads so quickly frightens most gardeners; they regard it as a threat. But the fact that it is so commonplace and invasive, doesn't detract from the fact that it has an attractive leaf or that it looks glorious when displaying its packed pincushions of creamy florets or the great bunches of shiny black fruit.

And, for the impatient gardener, it's ideal. It was the vigour which attracted me. I wanted something which would grow quickly to keep out the wind. And I knew that an afternoon with a pick would be enough to dig out shoots and seedlings and control any invasion.

It was speed of growth which attracted me to Myrobalan plum trees as well. 'There's no question at all, that's what you must have,' was Eric Barker's advice. 'You need something nice and thick for screening high up—between five and twenty-five feet—and Myrobalan plums are ideal for that. They grow very fast and, apart from the shelter they provide, in good years you'll get decent crops of delicious little plums as well.'

Advice from Eric Barker is advice from an expert—other growers have said that he knows so much about pruning that he could take his shears to a telegraph pole and make it bear fruit. So I took it. I bought five well-rooted 'whips' (which are six feet tall), in the hope that they would provide protection faster than the smaller cheaper trees.

The amount of protection which a hedge provides depends on its height as well as its thickness: roughly, a hedge will shelter an area three times as long as its height. So a twenty-foot tree should give sixty feet of protection.

With this principle in mind, we had ordered the Lombardy poplars at the same time as the Myrobalan plums. Apart from the fact that a line of them in the landscape always evoked memories of happy holidays in Italy, we hoped that if planted fourteen feet apart, behind the Myrobalans, their heads would ultimately meet at thirty feet above the ground to provide a high wind-screen.

At that time the western hedge above the house, with tall elm suckers and ash at the top, a good stretch of mature hawthorn in the middle and a large oak at the bottom, needed no thickening.

But south of the house, the hedge along the western boundary, was unsatisfactory. In places, elm sucker, ash and blackthorn were recovering well from what had been total decapitation some years earlier. There were also a few useful stems of laurel and one eight-foot-tall stump of an apple tree, which leaned at a crazy angle but had potential as a prop for the rambling dog roses which were firmly established at its base. Apart from that, the hedge consisted entirely of gaps.

On the other hand, it did have two marvellous features: its

width (up to twelve feet in places) and its plethora of naturalized narcissi, snowdrops, primroses, scillas and bluebells in spring, and fine dog rose, honeysuckle and wild hop plants in summer.

If we could fill the gaps quickly and put more plants in among the established shrubs, it would become the perfect mixed hedge—or 'medge', as Di and I began to call it. (Di was one of those slaves who threaten empires; she had begun to think for herself.)

I longed for something as lush as the wonderfully jungly edges to gardens which I had seen on the slopes of Mount Kenya. Di didn't.

'Seems a shame to miss such a wonderful opportunity,' she said in a slightly disdainful way. 'All you ever think about is thickening-up.'

'Well,' I exclaimed, 'you know what you did to the tractor drivers when the weather was fine.'

'All right, fill the gaps,' she replied impatiently. 'But why not try a bit of thinning here and there as well. If you change the density of the canopy you can let in more light in places, then you'll get more primulas and other woodland plants. Manage it properly, and you can have a miniature wildlife park and a miniature woodland garden as well.'

'She's right, she's right, it needs thinning,' slave Kirsten said enthusiastically. Kirsten was the demon of the secateurs, never happier than when battling inside a canopy of thorns. Draining her sherry glass, she gave it to me and rushed off for her gloves and shears.

To provide those areas of different light intensity, we pruned the existing shrubs to form a hedge which sloped gently up to a high centre and then gradually down again to the track. In places we took out shrubs on the lawn side and cut back the undergrowth to form miniature glades. Other areas where the hedge was thin were filled with individual shrub roses of the five varieties which we had also planted in the bottom hedge.

To create a high point towards the bottom of the hedge where it sloped away, we planted a Sumach which, with its odd furry antlers, wonderfully red foliage in autumn and prominent candles of berries in the early winter, would, we knew, be outstanding.

Where the gaps were widest we planted evergreen viburnums which, apart from being quick and thick growers, also have flowers and bright berries when other colour is fading, at the end of the year. Trying to provide more screen quickly we also planted common buddleia (which we knew would attract butterflies) and the delightful snowberry bush with delicate pea-green leaves and insignificant flowers which end up as snow-white, long-lasting balls to decorate the bare stems in winter.

Still not convinced that we had done enough to fill the gaps, I created a screen of wire mesh strung like a washing-line between the old apple stump and a strong stake. Planting a Clematis montana at the foot of the tree, I hoped that it would soon grow up to the wire and, using its mesh as support, rapidly cover it with stems and foliage.

When that job was completed the days were growing very short indeed. The enthusiasm of the slaves had waned. Most of them hadn't seen a decent film or play for months.

By the time they had reached their beds they were always too exhausted to even read a good book. It took most of the week in London just to recover from their weekend's work.

'You are brutalizing us like peasants,' one of them rebuked when I had remarked upon a distinct lack of enthusiasm for my weekend plans.

Realizing that if I was too insistent I might lose my vital labour force forever, I decided to call a halt to all work for the next eight weeks. After all, I reflected, in our first season we hadn't done badly.

From a long abandoned farmstead we had created the rudiments of a garden. Fencing and hedging had made our boundaries secure, and inside them some of the major features of a garden had been established. On both sides of the house there was levelled land sown with grass; thin, still, it only needed rain and aeons of cutting to become a svelte lawn. Sufficient young trees and shrubs had been planted, introducing more colour and variety of leaf to supplement those already growing on the land; all they needed was a few years of cosseting. One large and three smaller beds had been almost completely planted with flowering perennials to brighten future summers. Gravelled paths connected the main areas of the garden and there was even a primitive tennis court.

In review it was clear that the slaves had earned their period of winter hibernation, but I began to worry about the way to use their energies in future. The valuable work habit couldn't be allowed to wane for lack of stimulus.

Maintaining their enthusiasm would, I realized, be a problem. In the first year it had been easy. So much had to be accomplished everywhere so quickly that there had always been plenty of work for everyone. In future the need for more work would only become really obvious as the garden matured. Tasks would be undertaken piecemeal over a number of years. The whole time scale would alter. There would be dangerously long periods of inactivity before another burst of effort was necessary. Like a football manager, worried about maintaining the fitness of his team in the summer, I tried to envisage the future regime. Long walks and visits to places of interest in the vicinity would scarcely prevent the slaves from becoming fat and indolent. I rejected the notion of kite flying as being too sedentary; but I did decide to buy a set of metal French Petanque balls (which make you bend a lot) and some badminton rackets and a cylinder of shuttlecocks in the hope that those who loathed tennis might give these other healthy games a try.

Chapter Ten

I was sadly surveying that first winter's damage when the evil-looking mongrel sidled into the paved court beside the house. My heart sinking, I realized that Sneer would appear at any moment to depress me even further. He wouldn't pass up an opportunity to gloat—albeit with no apparent pleasure—that his pessimism had been so well-founded.

They say that owners tend to resemble their dogs. Certainly Sneer was just as unprepossessing as his. The two-day growth on his blotchy face and the lank and greasy remains of what had been sandy hair, looked as unwholesome as the dog's ungroomed coat, infested with mange and balding in places to reveal large patches of inflamed red skin. Above Sneer's ferret-sharp teeth projected a shark-fin nose, as perfectly designed for prying as the mongrel's dirty muzzle. And the whining, nasal, Birmingham accent echoed the dog's treacherous snarl.

It was surprising, in such a small community, that no one seemed to know anything about Sneer. A few people obviously knew who I meant when I described the bedraggled blue suit he wore, or his dog; but no one knew his name or where he came from. Clearly a loner, he shunned the village; he would appear—usually about three times a week—on the embankment of the disused railway from Uffington in the south and then, after pointing out my errors, disappear up the farm track towards the north.

Whatever Sneer's origins, from the outset I felt it was best to humour him. Whether he knew anything about gardening or not I did at least pretend to accept his acerbic comments with respect. I was so afraid of his potential for villainy that to please him I frequently bored slaves, who happened to be working nearby when he arrived, by repeating loudly the advice he had given.

'This gentleman says those shrubs will never survive the rabbits,' I'd shout across the garden with all the authority which I could muster.

'No chance, mate,' he'd confirm, nodding emphatically as he turned and followed his dog up the track.

They would never comment until he had gone. The girls found him frightening and creepy. Male slaves thought he was just unsavoury and could never understand why I encouraged him. For a while after he left their annoyance always made them moody with me. And I began to dread his frequent visits and the habitually pessimistic comments which he offered during our first summer.

On that day in late March, when he finally slouched around the corner, I was looking at the remains of our new flowerbed at the side of the house.

Although we had drained the water and closed the house for the winter, we had made frequent visits to the garden to try and complete the early planting. We had managed to finish two small brick-edged borders in front of the house and to plant them with a selection of perennials. Henriette and Doff had tidied the raised bed, which ran along the garden side of the paved court, by building a low wall at the edge of the paving.

The only benefits from all their hard work were those enjoyed by the rabbits and by Sneer. The rabbits had feasted well on the anemones, dwarf irises, and newly emerged hardy geraniums; and Sneer had the pleasure of seeing a disaster which he had predicted come to fruition. We had been warned of the increasing number of rabbits during the harvest, so we had covered the large herbaceous border with well staked down, small-mesh, plastic, anti-bird netting. Although it made the border look like an old lady's netted hair, most of the plants—apart from some precocious specimens which had prodded their way through the netting—had survived.

But, despite the warnings, we had done nothing to protect the other beds. Sneer could see from my sheepish look that he had scored a major success. But there were other triumphs for his pessimism in the rest of the garden so he did not, unusually for him, linger over his victory.

'I told you about them roses,' he said, his piggy eyes gleaming.

Gazing disconsolately at the ragged residual leaves and half-gnawed shoots of the line of twelve Queen Elizabeths, I didn't know whether to blame Martyn or the rabbits.

While by November in our first year the young Lonicera nitida cuttings behind the raised bed had become well established I knew that, as with all good hedge plants, it would take at least four years before they became a useful barrier. I wasn't prepared to wait so long to close off the northern and eastern sides of the court. The answer, I believed, was to plant a line of very vigorous tall-growing roses inside the Lonicera—they would provide an immediate temporary summer screen. When the Lonicera were established, I would be able to remove the roses.

We had chosen Queen Elizabeths because no bush roses grow so quickly. And although they tend to become rather leggy and bare at the base if they are not pruned hard, we used them in our previous garden and knew that they could easily reach seven feet in a single season.

Instead of attempting to gain height quickly by planting well-pruned bare-root roses, we had selected very tall container-grown Queen Elizabeths to plant during a warm spell in December.

On a visit to the garden with us at the end of February, Martyn had been very scornful. 'You can't leave them like that,' he declared. 'They will be impossibly thin.'

Before I had time to object, he pulled his much-loved secateurs from the pocket of his sheepskin and, with a few expert snips, removed ninety per cent of their wood.

'You won't recognize them in a month,' he said reassuringly. 'The sap is just beginning to rise, the worst frosts are over and you'll soon have strong new shoots breaking from the base.'

I was still dubious but he assured me that it always pays to prune roses just before they begin to make new growth. 'Then you don't have to cut out new wood which the plant has used a lot of energy in producing,' he explained. 'Most of the shoots which develop now can be allowed to grow on. You will only need to knock off a few of them—those which are obviously developing in the wrong place and would spoil the form.'

This was certainly sound advice for rose pruning in general. But by March I had begun to wish that he hadn't been so drastic, even though I knew gardeners are never supposed to 'spare the knife' when pruning roses. Looking at the remains, after the rabbits had feasted on the turgid new asparagus-like red shoots, I wondered whether, if some of them had been allowed to develop on taller stems, the pests would have found them less accessible.

Again, I was wrong.

In an attempt to survive, the roses put out further shoots which were instantly devoured. That must have happened at least twice more before, in a summer of very cool harsh winds early on, they finally died. Replacing them with another batch of tall container-grown Queen Elizabeths which I didn't prune, I found that they suffered the same fate. Our Vale rabbits, it seemed, browsed as skilfully as giraffes. When I mentioned it to Sneer, he replied, 'There's worse to come.' Even today, when the rabbits are at least under partial control, there are only five surviving roses of the twenty-nine in total which have been planted on that site.

The fatuity of planting delicate material until it is provided with at least some defence against birds, small mammals or insect pests wasn't the only lesson we learned from our first year's planting.

A wonderful show of spring flowers from bulbs long naturalized in the hedge south of the house, made us realize just how bleak the rest of the garden was early in the year. So the following autumn we bought two large bags of mixed narcissi for naturalizing in the grass along the foot of most of the other hedges. Similar bags, containing several hundred bulbs, are available for only about £10 and they represent probably the best value in gardening. Running a close second must be the long-handled planter we bought at the local ironmonger. It cut perfect holes in the turf for the bulbs and avoided hours of laborious bending.

Although the bulbs at first tend to produce their original rather vulgar large blooms initially destined for the cut-flower market, after a year or two they diminish in size and begin to look far more natural. The real bonus is that once settled into the turf they will reproduce themselves, putting out secondary bulbs alongside; so that after several years what begins as a lawn with a scattering of narcissi becomes a solid carpet of flowers each March.

Having originally chosen shrubs which would provide a good show of colour during the summer months—when we expected that the garden would be most used—we found that they too looked rather bare in the spring. So in the autumn they were supplemented by more evergreens and winter-flowering varieties.

But the great success of that first year of planting was the large herbaceous border.

When, in mid June, the slaves heard a visiting American cleric excitedly exclaim, 'Gee, you Brits certainly know how to garden,' they began to feel that all their efforts were justified. Even Lord Justice Mike, a questioning barrister capable of much contention (who had often rebuked me for my lack of logic in planning operations on colder days), felt compelled to use his talents as a photographer in trying to record the achievement. Looking at those shots today, I can understand why, for a few weeks, Sneer had no comment to make on the border.

The contours of the bed were splendid. Despite the chaos at planting time, we had managed to put the smallest plants in front and the tallest at the back, with the intermediate sizes in between. So that, as prescribed in all the books, the tall ones didn't mask the short ones as they developed. We had also managed to arrange that each variety of plant was placed in suitably spaced groups—three of each larger plant and up to five of the smaller subjects. This meant that there was sufficient foliage and bloom of each type growing together to provide a noticeable effect. The individual character of each variety compared to that of its neighbours was clearly expressed.

Since there was bright colour showing in all areas of the border at that time, we also seemed to have got the placement of the groups about right.

I was particularly pleased with the pinks. By mid June all their bluey grey foliage had fused to form fluffy mounds topped by a fur of pale pink blooms. Between them at the front of the bed many other colourful small plants prospered.

Behind, scimitar-leaved irises clustered like an advancing army, held their flags aloft like banners. Rich purple delphinium spires and the mauve, orange and deep blue candelabra of lupins helped to create a kaleidoscope of colour. Against the wall towering pale pink hollyhocks, high-rise verbascum, massive blocks of virginal white pyrethrums, stilt-legged gaillardias and one vast and jungly pink trumpeted mallow bush provided an exciting backcloth.

The impact was sensational. That is at least what we all felt in our second mid June. By mid July we were less certain. As the weather became warmer, colours faded and flowers withered. Despite Doff's mania for removing dead heads, the whole border became drabber and more untidy. Instead of self-congratulatory gasps of pleasure and minutes spent merely gazing in wonder at the fruits of their labour, the slaves began to ignore the border and took to croquet and tennis as a diversion. Glumly I realized that I had fallen into the flower gardener's worst trap. I had made no provision for a sequence of plants to display colour all through the midsummer dead season.

We had sown or planted very few annuals which tend to flower later. Apart from the need to remember to bother about them—always irksome for a lazy gardener who prefers to rely on perennials which require little care and attention—we rejected them because of our past experience of sowing seed in fine soil in the border. We had discovered that if the weather became too hot, too cold or too dry, the seed wouldn't germinate or progress until quite late in the summer, when the dead period was over and the later-flowering perennials were already beginning to provide good colour.

I knew that, with very careful management, annuals can provide a marvellous display throughout the dead season: that is most obvious in the gardens of some of the great chateaux, like the Nymphenburg Palace near Munich, most of whose visitors come in July and August. At the time I didn't think that the lazy gardener could ever hope to achieve a similar effect. Since then I have discovered, with the help of George Carter, Suttons Seeds' annual flower expert, that many annuals can be planted indoors in mid March and planted out as sturdy plants in mid May, to be in full bloom at the peak of the dead season, in July-August.

That is a technique we have subsequently adopted with great success. But more immediately we were able to repair the major deficiencies in our borders with the help of Alan Bloom, the herbaceous perennial breeder.

Bloom had been pioneering the use of what he called Island Beds—beds which visitors could walk round, seeing perennial herbaceous plants from every angle—at his idyllic Bressingham Garden in Norfolk. With no backing wall or fence, few of the established varieties of the taller plants used to create high points in the middle of the beds could, he discovered, survive standing up throughout the season without stakes. He realized that most amateur gardeners can't be bothered to stake their tall plants every year. The answer was to find varieties which, while preserving many familiar characteristics of the established breeds, were shorter. Some of them he had already bred or imported; others he set out to produce.

Thanks largely to his efforts it is now possible to buy smaller versions of many common border plants. Even lofty subjects like hollyhocks, verbascums and delphiniums can be bought in mini form. Not only will they stand up without stakes, they also take up less space on the ground, so you can pack more plants into a bed—which gives a better chance of a good spread of colour in summer.

So, during our second autumn, we replaced several of the bulkiest plants with smaller versions.

We had noticed, in the second summer, that while our irises had bulked up and flowered very well, they took up a lot of room in herbaceous borders and only flowered for a comparatively short time. And although there are smaller varieties of iris, we were reluctant to abandon the traditional large Germanica forms.

Again, Alan Bloom suggested a good solution. 'Choose a place that is not too prominent and pack all the irises into a separate new bed. When they are in flower they will draw attention to themselves. Before and after flowering their pleasant foliage won't be very obvious but will be quite attractive as a solid mass.'

Following his advice we moved all the Germanica iris and the Sibirica iris, simply planting their corms and bulbs at random closely spaced in a new bed on the slope up to the tennis court. To extend the season of colour in the iris bed, we also popped in a few narcissi bulbs and some foxglove seedlings. Trying to give the bed more character we planted a row of young globe artichoke plants to act as a hedge along its top side.

Firmly believing that a garden without foxgloves was a heresy to which even we couldn't subscribe, we had scattered packets of foxglove seed indiscriminately. 'They do well absolutely everywhere,' many people had told us. We were disappointed when their claim that 'soon you will have to fight them back like weeds' was shown to be false. No foxgloves appeared anywhere in the garden. Either the seed was poor, the birds were very hungry or conditions were not right for germination.

Unwilling to risk the absence of foxgloves for another season, we tried a different approach. We found one seedling in a hedge on the side of Brecon Beacon and were given several more by friends near Newbury. They seemed to enjoy their new home in our iris bed and, while we haven't had to 'fight them back', they are spreading slowly all round the garden.

Another beautiful weed contaminated the garden in that second summer: we were delighted to discover a royal purple variety of poppy. Nowadays their seedlings appear everywhere each spring. We leave as many as we can tolerate, since early in the year they are a real joy. Frequently, too, as in that second autumn, another generation (from the seed shed by the earliest flowers) pops up to gladden the season.

Doff, however, was showing less interest in the flowers: she had given up gardening in favour of civil engineering. Having read about Winston Churchill's bricklaying activities, and been inspired by the success she and Henriette had with the low wall they built alongside the tennis court, she had become more ambitious. She wanted to build a wall all along the eastern boundary between the cattle-shed and the top of the garden.

'Not too high,' she said. 'Just about four foot six—to give

us a greater sense of privacy and cut out the low wind.'

Since there was nothing but beautiful unbroken rolling country for at least twelve miles on the other side of the boundary, I was not too convinced about the need for privacy. However, there are times when it pays to agree.

When the simulated stone blocks were delivered, I regretted not having dismissed the idea on the grounds of cost. And just moving the ten pound lumps from across the gateway nearly provoked another slave uprising.

Determined not to become too involved, I hired a contractor to dig a trench along the boundary and pour in the concrete foundations eighteen inches wide and six inches deep, for the wall. Happily, as the weather cooled off, Doff lost a lot of her enthusiasm for building and decided to wait until the following spring.

When you are building a wall it is essential to lay a decent number of stones or bricks in a day so that they are all well set in the same batch of cement—otherwise there is a danger that faults will develop along the joints between different batches. I was doubtful about the number of heavy stones Doff would be able to move and set each day. But I was much more worried about the number of batches of cement which I would have to mix for her. With the exception of singling a field of turnips with a hand hoe, I know of no more laborious task than mixing cement by hand. Once wetted, cement and sand must be the heaviest material known to man.

I was contemplating the pile of stones and imagining the effort involved in mixing the cement, when I was suddenly inspired. Since Mike's strictures the previous year, I had become an avid reader of *Exchange & Mart*. I discovered that it is one of the world's great newspapers, because it is changeless and yet constantly stimulates the imagination. Every week its columns are packed with ideas. Small-holdings for sale in Cornwall conjure images of the tranquil rural life. Fishing boats for sale in Aberdeen promise, when converted, months of sparkling sea and sun cruising in the Aegean. Illustrations of fun undergarments provoke unmentionable erotic visions.

Stimulated by the thought of a huge pile of wet cement and

by the vague recollection of one of *Exchange & Mart*'s more unlikely offers, I was able to solve the problem of what to give Doff for her birthday. Unquestionably, what she needed was a brand-new, gleaming red, electric cement-mixer.

Chapter Eleven

It sounds like the teaching of an old Zen master, but it's modern wisdom from the school of experience. If you spend all your time looking at the flowers, you won't see what's happening to the trees. That is just what happened in our second summer in the Vale.

So much was going on in the garden that we seemed to spend all our time bending down over flower beds; we never had the time to stand up and look around at the landscape. The result was that I didn't notice any change in the elms until Sneer—as ever, the bringer of bad tidings—pointed it out to me in July.

'You want to take a gliff at them elms,' he said, indicating the pair of fine mature trees which towered over the meadow beyond the bottom of the garden.

They were typical of the elms in the stands which provided most of the nobility and grandeur in the landscapes of southern Britain at the time. We loved them because they provided an added excitement to the garden. The best views are those stumbled upon by accident—rather than presented too overtly—and this canopy of trees was like an enticing curtain which *almost* hid the White Horse. As your angle of observation changed when you walked across the lawn, the Horse suddenly came dramatically into sight. The estate agent who had sold us the house was not a man to appreciate such subtleties; he said, to our horror, that we could cut the elms down if we wanted to 'improve the view of the White Horse'.

Taking Sneer's advice, I went down to the south-west side to have a 'gliff' at the trees. Instead of the usual dull midsummer green, several boughs of both trees looked rather peculiar. The leaves were turning a dirty yellow and shrivelling. Some of them were being blown off in the strong breeze, as if autumn had arrived too early. I realized later that what I had been looking at were the first symptoms of Dutch Elm disease.

The tragic chain of events which ultimately brought the disease into my garden began in the almost insignificant traditional trade in Rock Elm timber. Imported from North America, this close-grained and extremely hard wood was the ideal material for making keels for small boats.

By 1966 many of the finest elms of all types in North America had been wiped out by Dutch Elm disease. It had been known for a long time that Ceratocystis ulmi—the fungus responsible—was transmitted from tree to tree by Scolytid beetles which are capable of flying several miles down wind. When arriving on a suitable host, fertilized females excavate galleries in the lower layers of the elm bark in which they lay their eggs. While doing this mining they pass on to the host tree the spores of the disease which they picked up from the infected tree where they first emerged.

When a tree becomes infected, the fungus quickly pushes its way into the vital sap tubes where, bathed in nutrients, it develops so rapidly that it fills the vessels and cuts off the tree's food supply. Starved internally, the tree quickly dies.

Two species of the carrier Scolytid beetles have been common in Britain since the eighteenth century. And the Dutch Elm fungus was identified here as early as 1922. However, while it was known to kill an elm from time to time, it was never considered to be a serious menace. Most of our British elms had proved to be highly resistant to the fungus. Sadly, most of the elms native to North America were not.

By 1966, while most of our elms prospered, vast areas of North American forest were mere graveyards of dead elm. It was probably in that year that a small consignment of infected Rock Elm was landed at Avonmouth Docks, near Bristol. Since the logs still carried their bark it is presumed that they also carried late stage immature forms of the beetle.

When the beetles became adult their first flight must have been into Gloucestershire because, in 1968, the Forestry Commission were asked to investigate a serious outbreak of a disease attacking elm in that county. The disease was obviously Dutch Elm, but the intensity of the attack prompted the Commission to investigate the fungus further. It turned out to be Ceratocystis ulmi, of a strain which had not previously been encountered in this country. And it was clearly frighteningly virulent.

At that stage there was no reason to be suspicious about the imported Rock Elm—the new strain of fungus could have resulted from natural mutation of a fungus already in Britain. But while the cause remained a mystery, the effects were soon dreadfully obvious.

A Forestry Commission survey in 1971 showed that Dutch Elm was attacking trees in three major areas—Gloucestershire and Worcestershire, southern Hampshire behind Portsmouth and Southampton, and Kent and Essex on either side of the Thames Estuary. It was estimated that more than 700,000 elms had already died.

The Government accepted the Forestry Commission's recommendations for emergency legislation. An Act was hurried through Parliament enabling local authorities to compel owners of diseased elms to fell them, and either treat the timber with insecticide to control the beetles or remove and burn the bark. The aim was to try and establish a 'cordon sanitaire', sealing off the infected areas and preventing the movement of the beetles into new areas.

At the time it was obvious that the main areas of infection lay around major ports; and although this strain of fungus had not been identified in North America, the Commission nevertheless began to examine imports very carefully.

The outbreak continued to spread and by the summer of 1972, when the disease reached my garden, a further million elms had succumbed. Attempts to control the spread of infection were unsuccessful: there were simply not enough of the highly trained professional foresters or tree surgeons with the sophisticated equipment necessary to fell large trees safely. By the end of that year the Government was compelled to repeal the legislation.

In January 1973, the vigilance of the Forestry Commission resulted in an important discovery. Examination of the fungus detected on an American consignment of Rock Elm landed at Southampton, showed that it was the new virulent strain. This led the Commission to conclude that the disease had initially been imported. But of course the ban on the import of elm (unless the bark had been removed) came too late to have any effect on the spread of the disease in Britain.

In fact, probably the only measure which could have prevented the initial outbreak from spreading would have been intensive aerial spraying along a band of land, several miles wide, surrounding the infected area. Apart from the cost, such an operation would no doubt have raised a storm of indignation from the strong conservation lobby—yet it might have saved twelve and a half million elms.

I could not possibly have imagined, as I walked back to the house on that July morning, what awful consequences the disease would ultimately have in our district.

Later that day, a very sad Robert Green stopped his Land Rover to confirm my fears about our two elms. Like all good livestock farmers he recognized the value of trees as protection for outwintering animals and young crops, as well as appreciating the elms for their beauty. Pointing to a hedge of elms which swept across the hillside to the north-west, he said glumly: 'I reckon they have gone as well.'

Even at that distance I could see the yellowing and shrivelling of some of the leaves. Within a few days many of the elms in that hedge and the two opposite our garden were quite bare.

We were pleased that Robert took down the trees as quickly as possible. Apart from the fact that the dead elms were a depressing sight, at that time we were still, naively, hopeful that such prompt action might prevent the infection of the remaining elms.

Our optimism was totally misplaced. During 1973 the whole Vale from Swindon in the west to Wantage in the east, became a veritable storm area for Dutch Elm. By the end of that summer hardly a healthy elm remained. And as far as we were concerned more than mere aesthetics were involved.

The wonderful hedge of mature elms, which ran away from our eastern boundary and protected much of the garden from the chilling north and east winds, disappeared in the plague. The four elms which were such a visual asset inside the garden also succumbed.

Since there were no large elms left to become infected there was no urgency to remove the large elm hedge. But we couldn't tolerate the sight of four dead trees in the garden and enlisted the help of Terry and a friend to cut them down. As usual he triumphantly overcame a difficult problem. We wanted the trees removing with a minimum disturbance to the other shrubs and trees which we had established nearby. The task was made more awkward by my insistence that they should only remove the crowns of the trees, leaving bare trunks sixteen feet high. I insisted because I am convinced that this is the best way to deal with a dead tree.

By removing the dead crown, the danger of the tree being blown down in high winds is avoided. But by leaving the trunk no nasty gap is created in the hedge and about eighteen inches of solid wind screen remains intact. Best of all, these totem poles can form a wonderful vertical feature in the garden—the Clematis montana and the Russian vine which we planted at their bases rampaged all over them. We were also lucky that the ivy lurking at the base of the hedge seemed to sense its opportunity and quickly began to compete, scrambling up to mask the bare trunks with foliage.

It was also Terry who made good the rest of the damage caused by the disease, providing a substitute screen for the giant elm hedge which had died.

Although Doff, as the proud owner of a red electric concrete-mixer, was the envy of all the female staff in the Department of Physical Medicine at Westminster Hospital, a year had passed without its pristine paintwork having been sullied by gravel, sand or cement. It wasn't that she didn't want to dirty such a lovely thing, it was just that she had to swot for exams during 1973 and didn't have time to start her wall.

After Dutch Elm struck, it was obvious that a wall only four foot six inches high would not be adequate to protect us from the chilling east winds. A much higher wall, up to nine feet in places, was required—a job which neither Doff nor I nor the slaves felt competent to tackle. So Terry was called in and, as usual, did a splendid job with bewildering speed. Even if he did chip the paint on the cement-mixer.

Where the elms which had formerly dominated our view to the east side joined the hedge, their suckers had helped to thicken it. Although we hoped those suckers might survive, the disease can spread through the roots and they all died shortly after the parent trees. Ironically this had the beneficial effect of allowing more light and moisture to reach a pair of lilacs, a yellow-flowered senecio and a potentilla which we had planted nearby, and they responded rapidly to the lack of competition, becoming much fuller in the next season and carrying more of their white, purple and pale yellow flowers. It was a wonderful lesson in the way in which shrubs can be held back if planted too close to established trees.

The loss of the elm suckers did however thin the hedge greatly, allowing us to see more than we wished of the new wall. We also missed the vertical features which the stems of the suckers had provided. It was when we saw the wonderful Moyseii shrub roses in Mattock's demonstration garden at Nuneham Courtenay that we knew what we needed as a substitute. Their robust stems, with thorns like jaguar claws, fountained skywards before falling back towards the ground. Three of them planted at the base of the legs of a five-foot-high wigwam frame (three lengths of wood stuck in the ground a yard apart and bound together with wire at the top) would provide excellent support for the young plants, and a solid base for the impressive thick mound which they would become in three or four seasons, John Mattock had explained. I subsequently realized that we owed the splendid froth of scarlet blooms in June and the dense clusters of vivid and highly decorative bottle-shaped hips in the autumn to the loss of the elm suckers, and felt agreeably compensated.

Even though the elm suckers had died in the eastern hedge we still had hopes that suckers in the western hedge—which formed such an essential part of the screen at the top of the garden—might survive. But we were again disappointed.

Although initially they seemed to develop normally, the buds bursting and bright new leaves showing, their sickness soon became evident. While the leaves continued to grow, nasty cracks began to appear on the bark of both the main stems and the tiny twigs on which they hung. We still kept praying for a miracle but none occurred. Having spread so bravely, the leaves gradually ceased to progress. And when they started to turn the pretty but slightly sickly yellow which we had seen so many times before, we knew that the suckers were doomed.

Fortunately the shrivelled leaves fell at a time when we were too busy just maintaining the garden to get round to uprooting the dead elm suckers. Otherwise we might have torn them out without realizing their value.

I was resting on the seat at the top of the garden, smoking beween bouts with the noisy mower and eyeing the dead suckers with jaded casualness, when I was suddenly inspired. The gaunt dead stems, with much of their bark gone and all their branches and even the tiniest twigs starkly revealed, looked just like the tall hazel cuttings which true cottage gardeners use to support their sweet pea vines.

We were using a particularly barren stretch of the tennis court surround net to hold up our sweet peas that year. But I knew that I wouldn't be able to use the same site in 1975 because, although there was plenty of rich soil at the foot of the net in which to dig the twelve-inch-deep, manure-based planting trench young sweet peas require, all members of the pea family can become afflicted by a sickness if planted in the same place more than once every three years.

The dead elm suckers would, I decided, provide excellent pea supports. But then, happily, I realized that I had been forestalled.

The mass of blackberry canes which had always tangled chaotically at the foot of the hedge and occasionally decided to invade its higher branches seemed to have become more adventurous. Instead of spreading laterally on to the edge of the lawn to seek the light, they had begun to climb the leafless elm. Instead of cutting away those canes which hung out over the lawn, I began to gently weave them back among the dead elm twigs. Despite the fact that their treacherous thorns ripped the skin of my arms and tugged at my sweater, I persisted for half an hour and was immensely satisfied with my work.

Realizing that this bramble weaving required a degree of patience and dexterity which only women possessed, I dragged two female slaves away from the more pleasing task of harvesting beans with the convincing argument that I was unfitted for women's work.

Despite their grumbling resentment as they bathed their wounds later that evening, they had done a splendid job. Dismantling my poor fabric, they knitted the bramble canes tightly together and, when they had finished, I could see that they had pioneered a promising technique of hedge rehabilitation which any courageous gardener could follow.

Today it is impossible to see the relics of the elm suckers behind the eight-foot-tall thick mound of bramble leaves in summer and barely possible to detect them beyond the thick tangle of woven stems in winter. I am certain that anyone who has lost a hedge (whether by disease, vandalism, insect attack, old age or simply a bonfire that has got out of control) which has brambles growing close by, could repair it rapidly with a bit of bramble weaving. And because the brambles are exposed to so much extra sun, the canes ripen large quantities of delicious blackberries.

I thought it was a brilliant idea. Sneer didn't. 'You'd have done better to plant briars.'

Chapter Twelve

The Chinese thought it was the year of the rabbit—for us, it almost was. But 1975 in fact turned out to be the year of the vegetable, a record-breaking year for the Rose household: we grew what we believe were the world's first £5 tomatoes.

Ever since the oil crisis of 1971 people had been digging for their own personal victories. You had to be self-sufficient. You had to grow your own. But we had only dabbled in vegetable growing: every year we had half a dozen tomato plants in two grow-bags, carefully located to catch the rain which flowed off the cattle-shed roof.

We didn't bother with the new, fast-maturing varieties like Eurocross or Moneymaker. We liked slower-grown plants of older varieties like Ailsa Craig which, although they might yield less, had far more flavour. Some years our tomatoes did well, some years they didn't—it depended on the amount of rainfall on the shed and the spells of sunshine. We didn't have much time to devote to them and we certainly couldn't drive down from London every day during the week to ensure that they got the two gallons of water they needed during hot weather.

I knew that they were pretty costly tomatoes. But I was an amateur, and an amateur tends to ignore the more mundane side of vegetable growing—the return on the money and labour invested, the opportunity lost of not growing something prettier—in favour of the deeper, philosophical aspects. Home growing, the amateur argues, is a healthier and more spiritually rewarding indulgence than womanizing, drinking or gambling. Nothing embodies more sensory satisfaction than the first boiling of pearly-fleshed new potatoes fresh from the earth, or the first taste of firm tomato still fragrant and warm from the sun. And that is a sound justification for the folly of giving them garden space.

Although I understand—and share—the desire to get 'closer' to the land, I have always had an ambivalent attitude to vegetable growing in the small garden. Vegetables are hard to hide. While they look marvellous in May when everything is green and burgeoning they are decidedly tatty and untidy in the autumn. Nothing could be more forlorn than a muddy half-cultivated patch showing the tired relics of a few sprouts or turnips in late winter. It was this reservation, coupled with the need to spend time establishing the general form of the garden, which made us late starters in the self-sufficiency race.

In the last year of casual tomato growing we had saved some money by using an office stapler and cheap sheet plastic to make our own grow-bags. But such economies were forgotten when I turned professional. I blame the insurance inspector for the disaster.

In January, a near hurricane harrowed its way across Britain, ripping out ancient trees and tearing the roofs off hundreds of homes. While we only lost a few dozen slates from the house and barn, many of the corrugated iron sheets covering the bottom bay of the cattle-shed were lifted off and dumped yards away in the field.

And it was the insurance inspector who said that when his company had paid for repairing the damage they didn't care whether we replaced the torn roof with corrugated iron or clear plastic. Taking him at his word, we converted the last bay of the shed into our alternative to a glasshouse—a vast airy and light protected growing area roofed and walled with corrugated Novalux plastic sheet attached to a wooden frame. It would have made an ideal studio for a sculptor. And it would probably have made an ideal tomato house for a better gardener than me.

It was certainly cheap—much cheaper than commercially available glasshouses—and any gardener with a garage, shed or outhouse that he can tinker with should consider modifying the roof before ordering a glasshouse. (And there is an even easier way of protecting a few plants with plastic sheet attached to a wall.)

As usual Terry did most of the fundamental construction, saving me money by using excellent well-seasoned timber bought from a demolition contractor. He wisely insisted that we spray it with an insecticide to avoid contaminating the property with imported woodworm.

When complete, my Novalux house sparkled encouragingly in the sunlight and positively invited the production of tomatoes.

Doff was impatient with my incessant calculations—number of plants, number of trusses per plant, weight of tomatoes per truss, cost of fertilizer, compost, etc.

'We're doing it for fun,' she insisted. 'I do wish you'd stop playing at being a professional.'

I couldn't make her understand that this time we were going to do it properly; the whole thing had to be costed. With enough plants, providing enough fruit, it could almost be made to pay. Somehow we had to recoup the £25 cost of the installation which I planned.

It was all possible, I knew, because some charming and ingenious people in Cheshire had produced what they called their Nethergreen Automatic Watering System. That was the key—we could spend the week working in London and grow tomatoes indoors in Oxfordshire, because the plants would get all the water they required.

A real expert advised me that he thought that most amateur gardeners would do well to adopt the ring-culture method of growing tomatoes.

Young tomato plants showing their first truss of flowers are planted on compost in open-bottomed whale hide pots. The base of the pots is nestled into gravel which is kept constantly moist.

To ensure that water was always available we decided to lay a sheet of capillary matting below the gravel. A tongue of the matting would draw water from a trough, which would be constantly replenished through the Nethergreen carburettor device.

Normally, in the ring-culture system the plant draws water up from the gravel through one set of roots and is fed, through a separate set of roots, from the compost in the ring on to which liquid fertilizer has been poured. Since we couldn't be there to ensure that there would always be enough liquid fertilizer, we mixed Osmocote slow-release fertilizer with the compost before filling the rings. This new fertilizer liberates its nutrients gradually over a period of nine months, to cover the whole life of a cold-house crop.

Since energy had become so dear we saw no point in trying to heat the growing area. Feeling that, like all but fanatical amateurs, we would be content to crop five trusses per plant, we planned to install the young plants in their rings in late March when the coldest weather had passed. We should then be able to crop through until mid October.

Again we were lucky to find what appeared to be good Ailsa Craig plants that spring. Within a few days of nestling the plants into the compost the first trusses of flowers began to set fruit and, seemingly happy in their new home, they began to grow. Even Doff appeared to approve of the final set-up.

It was Terry, normally such an encourager about the garden, who drew my attention to the problem a couple of weeks later.

'Of course, I don't know anything about it but to my mind that's tobacco mosaic,' he said pointing to some of the leaves. Instead of spreading they were beginning to curl and distort like arthritic hands.

Sadly, he was right. I will never know whether the young plants were contaminated with the virus (which also effects tobacco) at the nursery or were infected from my smoker's fingers. But within a few more days every leaf seemed to curl as it developed.

The disease is incurable but as the plant grows it slowly overcomes the attack and starts to develop normally. This happened with our Ailsa Craigs but it took until mid season. Meanwhile the fruit, which had set on the early trusses, either dropped off or hardly developed. Most of the flowers of what would have been the second and third trusses withered and in some cases no flowers appeared at all in the leaf axils.

When the fourth trusses appeared normally, I was greatly encouraged—even though by that time the plants looked so peculiar that I was reluctant to show them to anyone. The tomato house was large enough to store the lawn-mower and thereafter I was very scrupulous about keeping the door locked, so that the mower could not be stolen.

The ultimate disaster was caused by the myth that indoor

tomatoes need spraying with a fine mist of water to ensure that the flowers are pollinated. This is just not true: modern tomato varieties are so fertile and shed their pollen so freely that in most years the air currents, or insects just passing through, will almost guarantee pollination. But, being extra cautious, and labouring under the delusion that I was performing a vital task, I sprayed the plants.

The morning was much hotter than I had realized. Within an hour the sun had burned away a light morning haze and was beaming joyously. It was a marvellous day for cutting the grass so, after a morning's shopping and a snack lunch, I rushed down to collect the mower.

Disaster. I had delivered the *coup de grâce* to my tomatoes. The tiny droplets of mist, like miniature lenses, had so concentrated the sun's rays that all the delicate flower petals had been burnt.

There was no way I could hide the catastrophe, so for days I took a grim pleasure in taking visitors to the scene of the disaster to show them the narrow margin which separates success and failure in gardening. 'Nerve-wracking business,' I explained with vehemence. 'One false move and you are done.'

Such is the persistence of nature that a few fifth trusses developed on the bedraggled plants, and before the cold of autumn arrived five tomatoes actually ripened. Since they took such a long time doing so, their skins were rather tough. But Doff was kind enough not to mention it and declared them 'delicious'. I was grateful at the time that she didn't point out that, despite all my expert calculations, they had cost over £5 each.

I doubt whether we have recovered our initial investment yet; but having switched to the modern hybrid varieties—for the simple reason that they are never marketed until they have been proved to be highly resistant to diseases like mosaic—our crops have been much better in the last three years. We have found that a variety like Alicante, which can be fairly characterless if grown quickly in a hot-house, can produce fine flavoured fruit if grown more slowly in an amateur's cold-house. Especially one with an irrigation system like ours.

While I had carefully tried to hide the early disasters in my career as a professional tomato-grower, I couldn't possibly have kept the devastation in the rest of the garden a secret. Anybody could see what the rabbits were doing to my reputation as a gardener.

'What yer need is a rabbiter like my Split,' Sneer told me on several occasions, pointing to his vicious mongrel.

He didn't seem to understand that we couldn't leave an untended dog or cat on the premises during the week, and it was while we were away in London that the rabbits used our garden as a leisure centre. While *Watership Down* was germinating in the mind of its author, a few miles away in Wiltshire, his heroes were vandalizing my garden.

The annoying thing was that, while we often watched them scampering about the hedgerows in the early morning or just before dark, we rarely actually saw them in the garden. All we knew was that in our first four years they robbed us of well over £100 worth of young plants. At one time the impact of their weekday munching was so catastrophic that it became a joke. It was as though, as we drove away from the house on a Sunday evening or Monday morning, the bunny intercom invited them to a banquet. One of the slaves, to emphasize the point, callously pinned a paper to the bole of the oak tree near the gate which read: 'Plat du Jour—three dozen newly emerged Dahlias'.

When I told Cox's friend the sad story over lunch one day in a Soho pub, he nodded sympathetically. He was an older man, he had suffered for longer. I was seated on his 'wrong side' and throughout the meal he kept turning his head and pointing to his far ear.

'A little louder please, and on this side.'

When I'd finished and lapsed into silent despair, he put his hand kindly on my shoulder. 'You'll have to get a gun, old boy. But take more care than me.'

As I toyed with my pudding he told me about his personal battle with the more sophisticated but equally pestilential rabbits which had invaded the genteel residential area of Surrey where he lived. Like mine, his best rabbit sightings had been from the bathroom window. They had always disappeared by the time he reached the garden door, so he had taken to keeping his gun upstairs and firing through the bathroom window.

'Dreadful error, old boy,' he said wistfully. Apparently the shaving foam on his cheeks had stained the valuable walnut stock of his gun, and the din reverberating from the tiles in the bathroom had made him permanently deaf in one ear.

The 'Hungarian Hunters' model .22 calibre air rifle, displayed dark and sinister in the window of the local sports shop, seemed to promise less hazard. Almost silent save for the thud of its piston and the short hiss of expressed air when it projected the slug, it could be used without danger to the eardrums and wouldn't disturb lie-a-bed slaves if I saw rabbits from upstairs windows very early in the morning.

But before I bought it I tried milder remedies. The rabbits must have had a good laugh at the three-foot-high, wire-mesh fence which we completely enclosed the unwalled section of the garden. We very carefully dug it nine inches into the ground. It didn't seem to slow the rabbits down—they ate more than ever in the following week.

Furious at my failure, I sought the advice of the master of the pack of Long-Haired dachshunds.

'I'm afraid they'll only be using it for hurdling practice,' he said with a knowing laugh. 'You need four foot six to do any good.'

Fortunately he had plenty of wire in stock and kindly let me have enough to increase the height of the barrier by eighteen inches.

At least the new fence did have some effect. But it was by no means a complete success. Surprising a perky young buck with a large frond of lupin in its mouth peering out from behind a delphinium in the herbaceous border one evening, Doff and I gave confused and noisy chase. But even while I was rushing to grab the broken pick handle with which I was determined to kill it, the buck launched off down the lawn with increasingly large strides, scrabbled frantically at the corner formed by the barn wall and the inside of the fence, leapt almost sideways to its right and just cleared a shrub rose like a steeplechaser crashing through the top of the fence at Becher's Brook. We were frankly amazed.

But our astonishment was nothing compared to the shock we got when we returned a weekend later to discover that, at several places in the mini-woodland and at the base of other hedges, there had been serious efforts to establish real warrens.

Although myxomatosis had reduced the amount of warren making, it was clear that our garden didn't provide sufficient deep natural cover and the rabbits, which in our enthusiasm we had wired in, had decided to make themselves truly at home. Sneer was obviously delighted by the developments.

'You've made it too cushy for them, mate. Your fence is keeping out all the competition. Now the few stragglers who got caught inside have got it all to themselves. What you have done is to create a genuine rabbit reserve and only a ferret will get them out from them deep holes.'

The visit of the man with the ferret was a failure. Dropped into the mouth of several warrens in turn, the lissom minx-like creature reappeared with what seemed to be a questioning look in its bright eyes a few minutes later. I have no idea where they were hiding, but the rabbits had not stirred.

The ferret's owner re-asserted its alarming killer instinct. But when he dropped it into the first hole again without success, the ferret began to look positively disgruntled. It was expected to feed itself and was obviously hungry and disappointed.

When the rabbiter left, I wondered if he had seen and deliberately ignored another warren in the garden which I hadn't noticed. I had heard rumours that clever rabbiters—who depend upon the sale of rabbits as an addition to their income—never wipe out all the rabbits on any area of land. By leaving a few to breed and ensure a decent population in the following year they husband the rabbits carefully, ensuring both their sport and earnings.

'He could be farming the rabbits in your garden without your knowing it, mate,' Sneer observed, looking capable of just that sort of practice himself.

When I found a further warren among some thick ivy at the foot of the elm totems opposite the back door, I felt incensed and asked the ferreter to return.

'I can't,' he said. 'Someone has poisoned me ferret. When I looked in his cage this morning he was lying dead on his back.'

'Whatever would they do that for,' I asked, astonished.

'Dunno,' he replied flatly. 'Suspect they were jealous of my success.'

I hadn't the heart to comment or ask him whether he had

deliberately ignored the warren in the ivy and I put down the phone amazed, once more, by the depths of rural skull-duggery.

'Chemical warfare is the only solution,' one of my editors who didn't live far away declared with conviction. Grumbling about the difficulty which he had had in obtaining a licence to buy the highly toxic calcium cyanide poison, he lent me the forbidding tin with the admonition, 'For God's sake, be careful.'

Following the printed instructions I realized that I was handling a product of such potential horror that no amateur should be allowed access to it. The idea was to close off all the mouths of a warren except one by covering them with large turfs. Then, using a spoon attached to a long stick, the powder is inserted into the remaining hole. Then, that hole too is sealed with another ready prepared turf. In principle moisture in the air makes powder liberate the cyanide gas which kills the rabbits. Moisture in the respiratory tract of the person spooning in the powder would, unfortunately, have the same fatal effects.

That was a fate I managed to escape. And, after burning the old mac and gloves which I had used during the application, I drove the tin over to its owner and handed it back with considerable relief.

By the time I returned and made the rounds of the warrens to see that everything was in order, I found a series of freshly dug open rabbit holes alongside many of the turfs I had laid.

Discussing it with Robert he told me that the powder rarely worked on our sandy soil after a dry period. 'Either the gas must escape or there isn't sufficient moisture in the air to generate enough of it. Sensing it in the warren the rabbits seem to have time to dig themselves out and escape.'

Unwilling to borrow the dreaded tin of chemical again, I waited until after a good shower before calling the Ministry Pest Control Officer. He took the matter very seriously indeed and spent ten minutes over a pre-treatment cup of tea explaining the extreme dangers of the process. Before even handling the drum he pulled a dust mask over his nose and mouth and put on rubber gloves, a plastic mac and gumboots. Fully fitted out he looked bizarre on such a sunny afternoon. But we all refrained from giggling.

Through his mask he shouted to my father-in-law—a doctor—who happened to be staying, that the syringe and phials of antidote to the poison were on the back seat of his car, should they be required.

In view of all his precautions I couldn't understand why he chose to open the tin of powder right in the middle of the lawn on such a windy afternoon. Before he had taken out the first spoonful of powder, the violent air had started to stir its surface and drag out a thin spiralling plume. After staring fascinated to see how a real expert worked, I dashed up wind to avoid the danger. He was concentrating so hard on being scrupulously careful that he obviously didn't notice the cloud he was raising.

Less than half the tablespoonful of powder which he gingerly carried at the end of his outstretched stick actually reached the hole in the first warren. Most of it must have been deposited all over the foliage in the border on the opposite side of the garden.

Since he was the professional, I dared not say anything when he continued to seed the air with so much floating poison every time he recharged his spoon. I am not sure how we suppressed a laugh when, after so much earnest concentration, he smiled as he finished stowing his gear in the boot of his car and said happily, 'You just can't be too careful you know.'

Before beginning he had told us proudly that he was doing his last field job before being transferred to another Ministry to a clerical job which meant promotion. Obviously his superiors had realized that his talents lay elsewhere.

It was when it became apparent that his activities had been unsuccessful that I decided to resort to firearms.

Chapter Thirteen

Of course the difference between plasterboard and rabbits is that rabbits can run faster. Unfortunately Doff and I were so impressed by our marksmanship out on the rifle range that we had ignored this problem. Since we could regularly hit a piece of plasterboard the size of a saucer from a distance of twenty yards, we were, we thought, in the Davy Crockett class.

Sadly, the rabbits immediately spotted my weakness. If they sat still, they knew they were in trouble. So they ran. And while rabbits can look rather shambling and awkward while they are nibbling your garden, they are capable of astounding acceleration when they're escaping from a gardener with his gun.

'It's a .410 shotgun you need,' Martyn suggested. 'That will give you a spread of pellets and a better chance of hitting a moving target.'

Ever faithful, I thumbed *Exchange & Mart*. But I discovered that even in that cornucopia of bargains they were rather expensive.

'Why not buy my 12-bore?' a colleague at a press conference offered. 'It's an old hammer gun made in London years ago which I found in a stable. I don't need it now that I've moved into town.' He accepted a modest cheque on the spot and agreed to deliver the gun to a mutual friend whom he would be seeing the following Tuesday.

Dick Girling, a dedicated shot from the office, was intrigued: 'That's how they're always discovered, the old English hammer guns. They can be worth a fortune, you know.'

When I spoke to the mutual friend on the Tuesday, I was beginning to get excited myself. 'Yes,' he said, 'it's most impressive—lovely engraved country scenes on the metal.' The only bad news was that he couldn't deliver it to me until Friday.'

I was very impatient. A handmade English hammer gun with beautiful decorations! The rabbits were almost forgotten in the excitement. I might be able to retire on the proceeds of its resale. The three days before I saw it dragged dreadfully.

When it came I wasn't disappointed. Inside, the barrels shone as clearly as a healthy retriever's eyes. Outside pheasants burst from coverts and columbines entwined the finger guard. It was a beauty.

Some years previously I had interviewed William McKelvey, a director of Holland and Holland, considered by the discriminating to be the best gunsmith in Britain. He would immediately detect any minor defects due to age and might even make an offer on behalf of one of his wealthy clients, I thought.

His, 'Yes, I'd be pleased to look at it,' had me scurrying for a taxi. The taxi driver was intrigued by this long slim object I was carrying so tenderly. He couldn't actually see what it was because it was carefully wrapped in a striped bath towel.

Mr McKelvey is a very affable man. But this time I knew that the broad smile was more than just natural charm. There, I said to myself, is the satisfaction of a man handling something precious and beautiful.

'Black powder,' he said. I thought that sounded splendid. As I wondered exactly what it meant, he probed the barrels with a strange instrument apparently designed to measure the internal dimensions.

'Black powder,' I replied brightly.

'Afraid it won't take modern cartridges,' he explained apologetically, continuing to probe. 'Of course you can have black powder cartridges made. But they will cost about £2 each.'

That hurt a little. But it did not render the gun useless. 'Well, I don't propose to use it often so I suppose I could afford that,' I offered diffidently. There is something about the luxury of the firm's Mayfair showrooms which seems to make money an annoying irrelevance.

Continuing to smile, McKelvey went on briskly. 'Of course, you couldn't fire them through these barrels. They are out of proof—their walls are so thin that you would risk a dangerous explosion.'

Trying to be helpful he showed me the incomprehensible reading on the dial of his probe.

While I tried manfully to face my disappointment, he squinted at the decoration on the metal. 'Quite pretty really —make a charming ornament hanging above a fireplace— but if I were you I wouldn't do it—far too risky—some idiot will take it down and try to use it. And that could lead to a disaster.'

For a moment he stopped smiling and stared at me seriously. 'I'm very sorry but the best advice I can give you is to allow me to take a hacksaw immediately and cut those barrels up into small pieces so that they can never be used again.'

He allowed me a moment to register the dismal prospect and went on. 'You see we employ the finest craftsmen in the world. They can do just about anything—work in metal with such accuracy that while we talk about tolerances in terms of thousandths of an inch what we really aim to achieve between two surfaces is a perfect fit. But there is one thing which we could never accomplish.'

He paused. 'We have never successfully repaired a blown out eye or been able to rebuild the side of a face. And that's what anyone risks who fires this gun.'

Hoping that its antiquity might justify its renovation, I asked if anything could be done.

'We could reline the barrels but it wouldn't be worth it. It's only one of thousands made in a Birmingham factory and marked with the name of the London ironmonger who sold it.'

It was becoming clear that I would have no more success as an antique shotgun runner than I had had as a dealer in fine musical instruments. Sadly, I remembered the 'Stradivarius' I had found in my father-in-law's attic. My English hammer gun wasn't a Stradivarius either. Still, at least I might have saved a colleague's life by buying the gun.

The Greener, single-barrelled, Martini Action gun, which Mr McKelvey kindly found for me at a consoling price, is undoubtedly a more potent device. I have never fired it in anger but it performed very well at the company's test firing range.

Sadly, it lacks all the decorative charm and sporting appeal of the old hammer gun. The blackened serious barrel, culminating in a wider, perforated choke, would look good on an urban guerilla trying to effect a coup in South America; it would look terrible above a fireplace.

Perhaps a rabbit saw me brandishing the Greener in the garden, showing off in front of friends. Perhaps a message went down the bunny intercom. Certainly since that day I have never seen a rabbit while the gun has been in easy reach.

Chapter Fourteen

The lesson I learned from my battles with the rabbits is that defence is the best form of defence—especially when your attacks can only last for a weekend and the enemy's counter-offensive can go on, unimpeded, for the whole of the working week.

The fact that we were able, despite the attentions of all the birds and rabbits, to crop vegetables, had very little to do with the sustained fire-power of my Greener shotgun. It had much more to do with the fact that I had built Fort Knox to protect my most valuable assets.

Our Fort Knox is a cage, six foot six inches tall, with walls and a door made of small mesh wire to keep out the pigeons, tits, finches and other birds which will descend gleefully on young vegetable plants and demolish them as quickly as the rabbits. The wire netting, tough enough to withstand balls, barrows and bicycles, is supported by a frame rapidly erected from the slotted angle iron obtainable from most DIY shops.

The whole frame is topped by small mesh, lightweight plastic, anti-bird netting. Not only *can* this be easily removed in winter. It *must* be removed. The first winter after it was erected, our Fort Knox was badly bent—we forgot to remove the net and it collected six inches of snow in two hours during a blizzard. Under extreme stress, the uprights keeled over and sagged parallel to the ground. It looked as if it had been attacked by a gang of angry football fans.

I thought it would have to be dismantled for repair. Terry thought otherwise: he just bent the uprights back again with a rope and winch, and then reinforced them with timber stakes sunk into the ground and guy wires attached to the wall.

We had put the cage beyond the tennis court, so that it would be hidden from most of the garden. Sheltered from the north and east by the wall and the Leylandii hedge round the court, and from the worst of the prevailing west winds by the tennis court netting, it has proved an ideal growing area. Fairly open to the south-east, south and south-west, it receives the full benefit of any sun—an essential for successful vegetable growing. If the spot had not been so sheltered, I would have put up wind-screening material, hedging, or even wire or fibre-reinforced plastic sheeting. As it is, I am always conscious when working in the cage how much calmer it is than the rest of the garden and how much valuable heat seems to radiate from the light-coloured wall.

There is an appealing logic to the argument that home-growers should concentrate on growing exotic crops which are expensive in the shops—aubergines and mange-tout peas, for example. Sadly, the argument disregards economics and that most humiliating factor, the British climate. Only in years when the sun really flares—as it did in 1976 and 1977—can aubergines (which prefer a Mediterranean climate) be grown successfully out of doors. And while mange-tout peas will grow fairly well even in poor seasons, the plant produces so few pods that you need to give up a very large area of the vegetable patch to make growing it worthwhile. Which is precisely why they are so expensive at the greengrocers.

Experience has taught us that it is more satisfying to obtain a good crop of something ordinary than a poor crop of something exotic. From the outset we agreed that it was pointless growing main crop potatoes for storage at home—only once in twenty years will widespread crop disasters or searing droughts make that worthwhile. New early potatoes are another matter: they are always more costly in the shops, and even their best new potatoes never have the flavour of home-grown tubers cooked within minutes of being dug.

Since we so often seem to be on holiday when the new potatoes are ready to be dug, we have discovered that it pays to plant a variety which is equally good when left in the ground until the tubers are larger and more mature.

Our current favourite is the thin white-skinned Wilja—a variety from Holland which crops heavily and tastes wonderful whenever it is eaten.

Eighty seed planted at eleven-inch intervals in rows thirty inches apart, provides sufficient helpings to satisfy a family of four until the delight of the annual new potato experience has become a commonplace. In cooler areas it certainly pays to give the seeds a good start by placing them in a single layer on a tray with the eye ends exposed to encourage them to chit in a bright cool room.

The aim is to provide thick, short, dark green shoots, most of which should be rubbed off with the thumb, to leave only three, before planting at five inches deep. Chitting begun in the second week of March, should provide seed in the perfect state for planting by mid April.

The other crops we grow may seem unimaginative to the dedicated home-grower; but for a lazy gardener, it is a good annual programme: it produces decent quantities of vegetables with a minimum of effort. We grow courgettes—which are as undemanding as weeds and which, like the new potatoes, are still edible (as marrows) when they are cropped late—Webb's Wonderful lettuces, spring onions, radishes (all sown at intervals to provide a succession of salad crops), dwarf beans, broad beans, and two rows of an early maturing Fl hybrid sweetcorn (maize).

The sweetcorn is tender and full of flavour—although it is a miracle of plant breeding that one can grow it at all in Britain—and we find it does best if we sow individual seeds in small pots of compost in the glasshouse in early April and then plant them out, without root disturbance, in early May. It is also a tall plant and, planted near the edge of the plot, provides an attractive hedge. A permanent planting of raspberry canes is used as a similar hedge round the north and east sides of the cage—the raspberry canes are attached to the wire mesh of the cage for solid support.

To ensure a summer long supply of herbs, we have permanently dedicated two rows of the plot as a bed for perennial herbs like parsley, chives and marjoram to which we add a few sowings of annual herbs like dill each spring.

Avoiding the invasion of the other herbs by aggressive mint, we have established some roots at the foot of the

Standard Canary Bird rose and Hebe bush outside the garden, conveniently close to the kitchen window.

On the rest of the plot we try to rotate the areas in which we plant the individual vegetables and salad crops to prevent the build up of pest and disease problems. We take care to consider their relative position so that low crops are not shielded from the sun by taller neighbours.

We attribute our modest success as vegetable-growers to four major factors: good feeding, two methods of wind screening, and irrigation.

Each season we dig into the surface of the plot a thick layer of rotted cattle dung. (Spent hops, mushroom compost, or well-rotted compost would do as well, if we didn't have the stock of manure from the cattle-shed.)

At the beginning of each season we adopt the old timers' habit of providing vital low shelter for young and delicate emerging seedlings. We use a one-foot-high strip of polythene which we wire to the net surrounding the south-west side of the plot just above the ground to form a low wall. Even on the gustiest days we can see the leaves of the seedlings enjoying the sun, unruffled and calm.

To accelerate the early progress of any of the crops, we use an invention which we call the Super Cloche. Made very quickly from polythene sheet, wire and rough timber, it provides superb protection for young crops at far less cost per foot of row than anything commercially available. Its greater width and height allows crops to remain beneath it until they are very well advanced and until the weather is unlikely to become really cool.

The Super Cloche remains a fixture well into each summer, but with a seep hose laid alongside the rows of protected crops they can be watered without raising the plastic roof. We use similar seep hoses placed strategically along most of the rows in an arrangement supplied by Nethergreen to irrigate all our crops automatically at the turn of a single tap.

Another useful tip provided by Terry was the use of upturned wide-mouthed catering pack jars (glass or plastic) to protect individual plants which we wish to bring on quickly. They look peculiar but do work.

Sadly neither Terry nor anyone else could provide a satisfactory solution to a more intransigent problem which arose soon after the vegetable cage was completed. Once you have got moles, it seems, you have got moles and there is nothing to be done about it.

The soil was well dug just before the cage was erected and there were no moles around then. But by the time all the first winter sown broad beans had become sturdy young plants and the first dwarf beans were beginning to show through, the moles had obviously by-passed the eighteen-inch barrier of net sunk in the soil round the cage and begun to use it as their field headquarters. One morning there was just a hint of freshly excavated soil. By the next there was hardly a foot of the plot which didn't sport a Vesuvius-like eruption.

The fervour of underground mining had made many of the beans keel over at crazy angles, and at times had actually shifted them so far that it was hard to tell where the original line had been.

Happily, no one who gets moles lacks sympathetic allies or advice, but from our experience it is advice which can be safely ignored.

'Cut fresh bramble shoots and push them down the tunnels,' one said. 'Moles can't abide the thorns and they'll push off in an instant.'

Well they didn't. They simply carried on digging. The only result was that we managed to tread in some of the bramble and made it root in several places—it still emerges to trouble us today.

'Plant euphorbia—they never go within miles of a garden which harbours euphorbias,' the man from the muck and mystery school assured us at Chelsea Show. We didn't even bother to try that one because when we'd arrived the land had been full of it and in the areas which remained uncultivated many euphorbias persisted—some of them leaning eccentrically as the result of mole-mining beside their roots.

'Old beer bottles,' Sneer advised with a knowing look. 'Sink them up to the spouts and the wind blowing across their mouths will set up a whistle and vibration which the mole can't tolerate.' Apart from making the plot look like a garbage dump, pieces of the bottles (which the moles quickly buried and we subsequently shattered with spades) continue to cut our groping hands.

'This will finish them soon as spit,' said the Norfolk gamekeeper who, after long negotiations, had been persuaded to hand us a jamjar full of worms fed on strychnine. 'Just pop them into the tunnels and make sure you wear gloves and bury them deep when you are done. Don't on any account tell anyone where you got them because there is enough strychnine in that jar to poison the whole of Norwich and I had to sign the poison book to get it.'

Too terrified by his warning to risk scattering the currency of murder in our own vegetable patch, we gingerly popped the worms into the entrance of tunnels we found along hedgerows and covered them with heavy boulders to prevent people or other animals being poisoned.

Perhaps the tunnels we baited were the mole equivalent of slums, unused and awaiting demolition; whatever the reason, the worms did nothing to quell their activity and we have never dared shift the boulders.

It took more than a dozen telephone calls and a forty-mile detour to collect the children's celluloid windmills whose whirring noise and vibration in the breeze would definitely drive the moles away. One midweek evening en route for London I planted the ends of the windmill sticks into the soil as instructed. The windmills were effective in two ways: they made the slaves fall about laughing, and they encouraged the moles to even greater devastation.

Breaking out from the growing cage, they had burrowed their way all down the newly established orchard and begun to operate below the lawn. Judging by the number of mounds they created in a week it was clear that they were tunnelling out an underground version of Spaghetti Junction.

'If anyone makes better gopher gassers than these, please let us know,' declared the label on the American 'Mole Fuses' which, when lit and stuffed into the holes, would create enough smoke and gas to kill them 'painlessly and instantly'. So abandoning folk cures we embraced the science of chemical warfare. Matches blew out in the infuriating wind, damp fuses refused to ignite, many fingers were burnt and many fuses just puttered out when pushed into the holes. A few of them burst into life when brought out again and we breathed most of the gas—which provoked nasty hacking coughs which lasted for days.

About three of the gas generators worked correctly. Having

plugged the holes to confine the gas while it did its deadly work, we were about to make some tea when the whole lawn seemed to become alive with moles. Frantically burrowing their way out around the circumference of a circle centred on the fuses, five would get clear and dash away as the surface of the lawn began to quake at the efforts of another to escape.

It was like slapping the surface of a bowl of blancmange with the flat of a hand. Instead of being confined to a single cushy colony, the moles became active again everywhere.

The mole traps we resorted to resembled medieval instruments of torture. Two pairs of vicious teeth held delicately apart against a ferocious spring would snap close on any mole passing between them. 'But mind your fingers,' the ironmonger wisely warned. 'Those traps will bite like a tiger if you let 'em.'

It must have been beginners' luck. Of the two traps we bought, one began to shudder convulsively just after it was set.

My laugh of victory turned to a shriek of revulsion when I drew the handles of the trap from the ground. A fat mole mother, looking beautiful and soft and furry was impaled between both sets of teeth, but wasn't yet dead.

Trying to rationalize away the guilt I felt at the fate of this industrious creature whose long defiance I had inwardly begun to respect, I released her and crushed her beneath my boot.

Unwilling to face any similar episodes, I capitulated and accepted the weekly corvée of wheeling the barrow slowly round the lawn and shovelling up their fine, mined soil to scatter it on the flowerbeds before I mowed the lawn.

Finally, as the earth dried out and began to crack in the 1977 drought, the moles disappeared as quickly as they had arrived. Conditions in the moister meadows down by the river Ock must have suited them better, and they migrated. The diet of moles is mostly confined to earthworms and insect larvae. They too only become active near the surface when the soil is suitably moist and they can move through it easily.

The key to mole control is to apply chemical to kill the worms and insects during moist weather in spring or autumn. Then with nothing to eat the moles will simply go away—or so the real experts say.

They have come back again during the present wet winter. I don't suppose that we will try anything as drastic as the insecticide—in any case, the area of lawn they are mining is so large that it would cost a fortune. I suppose I will just have to get out the barrow and shovel again this spring. Unless, of course, I can make contact with that extraordinary lady near Gloucester who is said to have discovered the perfect solution. She sings Wagner arias at the moles. Upset by the quavering of her tremolo, they apparently just filter quietly away.

Chapter Fifteen

I was cutting the lawn without the grass box attached. In the strong breeze the clippings were scurrying everywhere like startled partridges. I really felt I was accomplishing something—there's nothing like practising what you preach, especially when it's a heresy.

Since it was dry I guessed that, within a few hours, the tiny fragments of leaf would wither and disappear shortly to become enriching humus deep in the mat of the turf. But even if it rained, I wouldn't care. The swath of clippings would take longer to dry out. They might start to rot on the surface and become unsightly or even hang about long enough to make the mown turf below become yellow. But they would soon vanish. Britain's climate is so wonderfully variable—few days pass without wet turning to dry or calm becoming windy—that it is always on the lazy mower's side. It's hard to stop grass growing and recovering after rain.

Happily it had stayed dry enough in 1976 for a drought to be declared. Grass growth was halted, mowing seemed obsolete, and a huge surplus was created in the lawn-mower industry. Which was how I managed to get a large discount on the 'hardly used' demonstrator model just before the autumn rains. It must be one of the world's widest single-cylinder mowers—a great crude chopper powerful enough to clear forests, its 32-inch cut has saved me hours of boring mowing. It came with a vast fibreglass clippings box which, because of my 'let the clippings lie' philosophy, I have never used.

I've probably never used the full 8½ HP the engine produces

either. But the machine has taught me that power is the key to successful mowing—sufficient power to cut even soaking wet and long grass without overtaxing the engine. All the other mowers I have owned have been reasonably cheap but dreadfully underpowered and therefore bad value.

Critics of my 'let the clippings lie' school of thought had warned me that my lawn would become infested with weeds: the seeds which would normally be carried off the cut surface in the box would remain, and germinate, in the lawn. That may well be true, but I fail to see how weed infestation can ultimately be prevented. No matter what grasses are grown, after a few years most domestic lawns will be packed with the grasses whose seeds have arrived there naturally and prospered because they enjoy the conditions. Most of the weeds are fairly discreet, lie prone like clovers and look very pretty. If they become at all offensive, a dose of lawn weedkiller will suppress them for most of two seasons.

They certainly didn't seem to have become much of a problem when I surveyed the effect of my efforts after putting the mower away on that late September day.

I was particularly pleased with a new patch of lawn on an area which had formerly been a gravel car park. Although less than a month old, the young grass plants had begun to tiller well and were thickening nicely. Copying George Cawthray, the groundsman at Headingley—the home of Yorkshire County Cricket—I had sown a new variety of grass from America called Manhattan. Its breeder, Doctor Reed Funk, had discovered some of its small but tough parents in Central Park, New York. He felt that if they had stood up to 300 years of trampling by New Yorkers they must be all right. In any case, if Cawthray thought it good enough for the Test Match square—he liked it 'because it kept its head down and didn't need so much mowing'—that was all the testimony I needed.

Its progress in a month certainly vindicated me in my belief that the best way to create a lawn is by sowing fast-establishing varieties of grass. Laying turf is an expensive and risky business—it's difficult to tell just how good the grass is —and it doesn't provide a useable service any more quickly.

Happily, new and scientifically bred grasses are emerging all the time and if I hadn't chosen Manhattan, a new dwarf ryegrass like Sprinter or Pencross (from the University of Pennsylvania) would have done just as well. Ian Greenfield, the expert in golf course construction, has shown me greens in use by golfers in the July which were only sown, with pure Pencross, the previous autumn.

Despite my pleasure in the progress of the new grass, and the feeling of spruceness which cutting a lawn always gives to a garden, I felt that there was an indefinable something missing. Until then we had been so self-congratulatory about our efforts in transforming a farmyard wilderness into something resembling a garden, that we had become blind to its defects.

'Still a trifle bleak, perhaps,' Faber had meekly suggested. He knew that I was sensitive and didn't want to make his criticism stronger than that. I sprang to the garden's defence. Pointing to the trees and shrubs which after five years were becoming quite established, I said that they'd soon give the place a better clad look. Faber hastily agreed.

I emphasized the astonishing growth of the Leylandii hedge round the tennis court. It had grown so well that we had just planted four apple trees in its shelter on the south side—a Cox's Orange Pippin and an Egremont Russet as late maturing and flavoursome desserts, a Laxton's Fortune as an early dessert, and a Lane's Prince Albert for cooking. I pointed out that we had chosen standards with tall main trunks which, although they would be difficult and need ladders to pick when mature, would nevertheless be far handsomer trees than the more popular half standards or bush trees and would, in a few years, be strong enough to support a hammock. (That idea must have lodged in the back of Faber's mind, because he provided a beautiful Mexican hammock at Christmas.)

'When the chequerboard is really set that, too, will provide more variety of surface,' I pointed out.

Some weeks earlier I had begun to realize that plain lawn can be very mundane. It's all right when it spreads over several acres. Then it is probably studded with noble trees and broken by shrubberies which have acquired the status of small copses. Such a lawn can be a wonderful screen for the shadow play of twigs, foliage and clouds. But just flat, relatively small and surrounded by low hedges, plonked down because it is the custom, lawn is boring—like a playing field without players or the tamed and tedious wasteland spread round the less imaginative type of housing estate. I suspect that careful research would reveal that the glassy light reflected by these barren sheets in sunshine contain wavelengths which are positively irritant and cause the head to ache.

Hoping to produce something more agreeable, I decided to experiment with building a pattern into the turf at the time of sowing. My efforts were confined to creating a chequerboard of adjacent one-yard squares of lawn sown with two separate varieties of grass whose leaf-shape and colour were so different that they would show up as a clear pattern for several years. Our trial was restricted to a patch of twenty-five squares over the old car park. We sowed pure Agrostis stolonifera, a Pencross variety, and pure Festuca longifolia, Hard Fescue, squares on the advice of Jonathan Franks, British Seed House's turf expert.

While in a few more years the crisp edges of the squares will disappear as the grass varieties spread into each other, there is no doubt that the surface of that section of the lawn will be interestingly dappled for a long time to come. Instead of a chequerboard, we might equally well have chosen a diamond pattern or even stripes.

But my arguments had only half convinced Faber. More to the point, they had only half convinced me. I shared his doubts. And they were doubts which lingered, unresolved, throughout the winter of 1976-77.

Instead of diligently pursuing my work at the office, every spare moment was spent in drawing sketches of the garden. The view from the front of the house, which had been so satisfying after the lawn had been established, now seemed to have become bald and obvious.

It took me a long time to realize that the death of all the elms in the Vale had substantially changed its character. Our view was different: still beautiful, but more open. And that meant that we were more dependent upon what we planted ourselves for a feeling of leafy enclosure.

A fortnight before Easter, when the slave labour market would open for the season, I was still desperately trying to decide how to deploy their energy to solve my problem and had been sketching for most of the afternoon.

I was making yet another attempt when a shadow fell over

the paper. It was my editor, Philip Clarke. He had been very long-suffering but I knew that even his infinite patience had bounds.

'That's lovely. But where's the copy for your article?' he enquired with a frown.

'Just waiting for a final phone call before it's complete,' I replied guiltily.

'Well, I need it by 10 am tomorrow at the latest. You are starting to hold things up,' he said with a resigned shrug.

I had been muttering about the problem for weeks while trying to keep up with his giant strides as we walked to the pub at lunchtime or to Chancery Lane tube station in the evenings.

He was about to return to his desk when he leaned over my sketch and looked at it critically in silence. And then what I had been hoping for happened. I needed someone with his unusual flair and imagination who could come to the problem fresh. He had never visited the garden, only seen some photographs and my sketches. But I knew that he was an enthusiastic and skilled gardener himself. Instead of continuing to chastise me about work, he rushed back to his own scribble pad and launched an attack on the problem.

A few minutes later he called me over and thrust the pad towards me. 'That's what you must do,' he said firmly. 'All your present lines lead the eye right out of the garden. You have got to change them so that it is led right back again.'

What he suggested was gradually curving the corners at the bottom of the lawn and planting two small shubberies in the areas which would be outside the new lawn edge.

To make the lawn shape more interesting, he also thought that we should extend the main herbaceous border right up to the house and create a small curved-edged bed at the north-west corner of the lawn.

'Sheltered by the hedge it must be very dry there. You could plant some of Beth Chatto's wonderful euphorbias and make one of her spectacular giant cardunculus thistles a major feature.' During the previous summer we had visited Beth Chatto's wonderful garden near Colchester together and become ardent fans.

I was fired with enthusiasm by his suggestions. On the Good Friday I used the lawn-mower to define the gradual curves for the new lawn edges in the uncut grass. With such a big and cumbersome machine it was important to avoid curves which were too tight and difficult to follow. I wanted curves which were easy to mow and discovered, as I was cutting them, why curves are not often very satisfactory in a small garden. Curves that are too tight look fussy, not interesting; they need a lot of space to develop gracefully and read properly. When I had finished, I thought that mine looked fine.

Determined that the proposed new plantings should be accomplished over the holiday weekend, I left a group of slaves under Faber's guidance digging up the turf on the area which would become the new herbaceous beds. Meanwhile, I rushed off to seek Mike Tucker's advice in buying a collection of shrubs and herbaceous plants which had been grown in containers.

On my return I was astonished by the progress which had been made. The form of the new beds was clearly visible in newly exposed soil and the barrow was working overtime ferrying the stripped turves away. Enlivened by two bottles of sherry, the slaves were as noisy and gregarious as a flock of barnyard hens.

They had been joined by 'Whirlwind' Dickie Waugh fresh back from Saudi Arabia and his wife, Hazel, who had motored over from Ramsbury for lunch. As good at 'getting on with things' in the garden as Martyn was at 'doing-up', they had created several fine gardens in the region—and two in the Argentine—in the few years since we had known them.

When she saw the load of plants I had lined up outside the back door, Doff was irritated. 'Now we'll never get them in for lunch,' she groaned.

But I was keen that the slaves shouldn't be allowed to lose their enthusiasm and momentum. Waugh had already hurled aside his Norfolk jacket and his smart suede shoes had become covered with the soil scattered in his furious digging. Working with equal vigour alongside him, Hazel looked distinctly odd in a splendid 'going-out-to-lunch' suit and outsized gumboots.

Work wasn't completed before lunch. But by the time we drove back to London on the Easter Monday night the new beds had been dug over, had a good dressing of the old manure and had been garnished with well-watered-in plants. Even the shrubs were in place and the whole garden seemed to have acquired a new and more exciting shape.

It was a perfect example of the rewards which gardening can offer. So often in life plans are frustrated. Months of work can end in projects being abandoned. But in gardening things are different. With enough willing helpers and today's aids to instant gardening, like well-grown containerized plants, whole landscapes can be satisfyingly transformed in a few days.

Chapter Sixteen

The sleeping car attendant on the Aberdeen-London train seemed very distant when he checked my ticket. Perhaps the scramble of seventy-five-feet of one-inch sisal rope spilling out around his legs from underneath the berth upset him. Possibly his regular first-class gentlemen didn't try and transform the compartments into ship's chandler's storerooms.

He had certainly been upset when, sweating up the platform with the giant coil on my shoulder, I had refused his offer to put it in the guard's van.

But it had taken me weeks to find such beautiful rope and I didn't dare risk losing it. Many times I had been offered half-inch sisal rope; but when I insisted on something thicker—everyone brought out brilliant blue-white nylon. No good at all—I needed rope of an impressive dimension which looked natural, because I was going to create a screen of rambling roses along three strands of rope, strung between four fine, eight-foot-tall oak posts which Terry had set behind the herbaceous bed in a line between the house and the barn. I didn't want something that looked like a washing-line.

Since I was in Aberdeen on business, I thought I would take the opportunity of visiting a chandler who supplied trawler skippers. And he had just what I wanted. All I had to do was to get it from Aberdeen to the Vale of the White Horse.

I should have told the sleeping-car attendant the whole story, why a visit to the gardens of the Alhambra Palace in Granada made it necessary for me to share my compartment with a pile of smelly rope. Or why my early experiences with a water garden in Calcutta and more recent pleasure in Mary Wakeman's water feature in her garden on Martha's Vineyard Island, Massachusetts, had me crazy about water. But I was exhausted after an exciting day hearing about rose breeding from Alec Cocker. And I suspected the attendant didn't have the time.

His, 'Aye well, I'll bid you guid night,' when I refused his second kind offer to take the rope to the guard's van was proffered with the tired resignation of a man humouring an imbecile.

He left me staring in excited anticipation at my rope. I could imagine great swags of it thickly clad with the entwined stems, foliage and blooms of the fast-growing Kiftsgate roses which I planned to plant at the feet of the posts and train on to the rope. This living screen would, I hoped, make it difficult to see what lay beyond.

And behind it was to lie my water garden. This was what I had brought back with me from my visit to the magical Generalife gardens of the Alhambra Palace. The inspiration of that superb garden, with its michievous use of water and the subtle visual tricks achieved with walls, arches and courts, glimpses and surprises, excitement and calm, could not just be left behind. Some of it had to be brought back to the Vale.

Flushed with the success of having found the rope of my dreams, I went to sleep that night anticipating the triumph of my water garden. I was going to capture the elusive atmosphere of the Generalife, I vowed.

I couldn't understand why I felt so drugged or why my tongue tasted of burnt varnish when the attendant woke me with a cup of coffee.

'That stuff certainly stinks, sir,' he gasped. I suppose, from his disapproving look, that he was worried about the effect the smell might have on the gentlemen taking the sleeper back to Scotland that night. His anxiety was justified—the compartment reeked of processed sisal. As I sat up to take the tray, my head reeled. This sisal was powerful indeed—I began to worry about glue-sniffers moving on to this harder stuff.

Luckily the effects of my sisal overdose had disappeared by the time the train arrived at Euston. I had returned at the weekend, so I trailed my bag and my rope down into the

Underground, round to Paddington and on to a train to Oxford. There an astonished Doff—she had spent the week in the Vale with her father—met me with the car.

When we reached home my father-in-law was standing in the courtyard looking down towards the barn, so rapt in concentration that he didn't notice our arrival. He was slowly rolling a cigarette from one corner of his mouth to the other, taking an occasional puff. With hands on hips and arms akimbo, he slightly bent down twice to take a sighting from nearer the ground. It was a performance I'd seen before, just prior to a difficult putt, and it embodied all the intensity of concentration possessed by a man who had twice won his county's amateur championship.

He was critically examining our latest developments. First, the line of tall posts which would take the rope I had just dragged out of the car; then, for longer, the cement foundations for the water garden. They looked pretty messy.

I had long been conscious of the dead patch of garden to the east of the path from the house to the barn. After seeing the gardens of the Generalife and being inspired to create a water garden, it was the obvious place to put it.

I didn't want the usual small and deep plastic or cement-lined scummy pond. I wanted long stretches of water to emphasize vistas, to reflect the colour and changing moods of the sky. The simple way to achieve this effect cheaply was to create a maze of very shallow (six-inch-deep), narrow (eighteen-inch-wide) canals with occasional wider ponds to make the system seem more extensive, and two deeper (eighteen-inch-deep) sumps to house plants like water lilies which need that depth. To provide added interest I wanted several levels, so that the water tumbled gently over weirs.

Since hundreds of plants grow well in shallow water, I planned to fringe the edges of the canals with them to mask the cement walls. Other beds alongside the canals would house plants whose foliage hung over the walls, to complete the camouflage. I also planned to create a moist bog garden alongside the main pond, with a very rocky dry bed close to it. The silvery foliage and white flowers in the dry bed would contrast strikingly with the lusher, sour greens of the bog plants.

Water garden from the south

1. Giant's coffin raised bed
2. Canalside beds
3. Cairn
4. Dry bed
5. Roses on suspended ropes
6. Top pond
7. Bog garden
8. Sump

And by May 1978 the whole conception was fairly successful. But in the previous summer, while the system was being prepared to take water, it made a very nasty harsh scar in what was otherwise becoming quite a pleasant garden.

Pa-in-law was a bit embarrassed to realize that we had been watching him and came forward to greet me affably.

I nodded towards the waterworks.

'Yes,' he said rather shyly inhaling a deep puff of smoke and pausing, 'Yes, at first glance I thought you were making your own sewage works.'

Anyone who makes a living out of writing soon gets used to receiving no encouragement from their family.

'However,' he went on, still looking rather doubtful, 'I expect it won't be too bad when it is planted.'

I had been so mesmerized by my own vision of the water garden as a mini Generalife that there had been no room for doubts in my mind. But his reservations rankled. I knew that he was a talented gardener and previously I had always valued his advice.

It would be awful if he was right, I thought. Terry had lovingly laid such a vast area of cement that it would be extremely difficult to obliterate if the scheme was a failure.

My haste to discover whether the design would work led me to commit the water gardener's greatest error—buying the plants before the system has been proved leakproof.

Terry confirmed over the telephone that the water-proofed cement lining had been applied by the Wednesday and that I should be able to fill the system by the Friday evening.

Detouring via a Hertfordshire water garden centre I bought a massive load of compost, planting baskets and water plants, plus a submersible pump. The pump was to be stationed at the bottom end of the system and would recirculate the water via an underground pipe to emerge as a gently flowing spring from a cairn of rocks at its head.

Although it was nearly dark when I arrived, I immediately began to fill the system with a hose and scattered a thick layer of attractive gravel over the cement canal and pond bottoms. The aim was to dissolve away any noxious chemicals from the cement lining and gravel in the first filling. This would be drained away on the following morning before refilling with fresh water.

It was nearly midnight when I finished and the system was full. Turning on the pump I was enchanted by the noise of the gentle trickle from the spring in the calm night.

Walking back to the kitchen door on my way to bed, I paused and looked round at the system again. The main canal along the garden path shimmered magically as it reflected the courtyard light. And, to my joy and astonishment, I realized that a harvest moon like a giant orange had just broken clear of the White Horse hill and was being reflected as a glittering disc in the gently ruffled surface of the upper pond.

'That's it,' I cried aloud, dashing upstairs to get Doff out of the bath to witness the glorious spectacle from the landing window.

I was much less enthusiastic when I glanced out of the same window the following morning. The system was half empty. I was frankly baffled. Perhaps the water-proofing cement was old stock and had become defective. I still don't know because even when I had siphoned out the remaining water and laboriously swept up all the gravel I could find no cracks.

It took much of the morning to get rid of all the water and sweep the cement clear so that it could dry. And by that time it was very hot. Pausing to rest, I realized that I was about to face a disaster. All the water plants which I had bought on the previous day were standing along a wall in full sunlight and beginning to flag dreadfully through lack of water. Fortunately some slaves arrived quite soon to help me carry them to the shaded eastern wall of the barn. As we moved them, those with the most delicate foliage seemed to be turning brown and smelt as though they were beginning to rot. The only hope was to arrange for someone to spray them thoroughly every half an hour. Otherwise they would not survive.

I was contemplating the fact that through my own folly I was about to lose over £50-worth of plants, when Imogen arrived to suggest that I drive the six miles to Hinton Parva to buy plastic pond-lining paint at the water garden centre. I didn't know whether to be grateful or to scream. My trip to Hertfordshire had been quite unnecessary. I could have ensured that the pond was leakproof and then bought the plants at no distance from home. If only I had been more patient I could have avoided all the angst.

Keeping the plants alive during my subsequent week of holiday turned out to be a true corvée. I needed dry weather for treating the pond lining but longed for rain to spare me the task of hosing. Even just a dull day would have reduced the burden. But each day dawned brighter than the last.

A single coat of pond lining proved inadequate to staunch the invisible leaks, so a second coat had to be applied and it was Friday—a week since the plants had had their roots in water—before the system could be finally filled and they could be arranged along the canals.

Many more of them survived than I deserved, so that by the autumn they looked quite pretty. I had planted them in a special peaty compost in sloping-sided plastic baskets. The compost was prevented from spilling through the slots in the sides of the baskets (designed to allow uninhibited root growth) by lining the baskets with a sheet of hessian which rots away after the compost has settled and become root-bound. To disguise the baskets and hold the top of the compost in place, I buried them in mounds of the same gravel which I used to cover the canal bottom. Since my lily troughs were too narrow to take the proprietary plastic buckets, I improvised by making two from metal rabbit netting.

By the time Pa-in-law saw the water garden in the summer of 1978, it was quite well established. Very little of the cement lining was showing. Plants in the bog and dry land areas had thickened-up and many of them were in flower. The whole area positively glowed with the white, pink and scarlet blooms of the pinks which we had obtained from the late and memorable Mrs Desmond Underwood's Colchester nursery and had planted in the beds alongside the canals. They contrasted beautifully with the quite different colour and forms of the plants pushing up from the water. Pa-in-law was generous enough to smile his warm approval and particularly appreciated the heavy perfume from the pinks at night after they had been cooked all day by the sun.

He was, however, as depressed as we were by the Golden Orf which buggered orf.

When preparing an article about animals in the garden, the

expert I spoke to insisted that there was only one species of fish to buy. 'Golden Orf, old boy,' he had said with absolute authority. 'They are a must, so much nicer than shy goldfish, they just can't help showing off—even a snatch of sunshine and they are hovering about on the surface practically eating out of your hand.'

Well he was the expert so that's what I told the readers. I don't suppose that those who took the advice have forgiven me yet. I can only conclude that the man gave me the wrong name in error, for while the dozen Golden Orf we bought glinted an enchanting reddish gold in the plastic bag on the way home, we have only caught fleeting glimpses of them on infrequent occasions since they were freed in the pond. And what we have seen hasn't been very pleasing. They have grown all right—though they must have devoured the expensive high protein food we fed them under cover of darkness. The sad thing is that they have lost all their baby charm and, as my step-daughter said cryptically one day to emphasize the value of a wide-ranging education: 'They look like slightly obscene and very overgrown carrots.'

Trying to provide more visual grace, she and Pa-in-law came back from a secret mission with two perfectly normal and very lovely goldfish. They were christened Gert and Daisy because they seemed so fond of the limelight. Their frond-like swaying gave us hours of pleasure even before they proved that they had been misnamed and produced twenty-five spritely offspring.

Having decided at the Generalife that, like women, the most attractive gardens are those which conceal their charms, I decided to try to make it even more difficult for the whole garden to be seen from any one place.

It was Doff who suggested the most useful barrier to vision —a wall across the south end of the courtyard broken by a wide archway to lighten the effect and provide access to the barn and the front area.

Terry could attach one end of the seven-foot-wall to the house. But to strengthen its eastern end he suggested that we change its direction by ninety degrees and run it south for a couple of yards. It turned out to be another fine idea because it created a sheltered hot south-west facing corner in which to sit and enjoy the water garden. The brick and wood panelled wall could quickly be hidden behind the foliage of Clematis montana led on to from the side of the house.

There is another Moorish feature in this part of the garden: an arch, cut out of the thick fronds of the Leylandii hedge, which provides access to the orchard. It echoes the round top to the front door, the arch in the courtyard wall—and the round-topped windows of the barn. A great find those—I salvaged them from the old Army and Navy Store building on Victoria Street when it was demolished, and triumphantly transported them down to the Vale knowing that they were just what I needed for the barn. Luckily they fitted in the car. I wouldn't have wanted to try taking them by train.

Chapter Seventeen

The remarkable thing about actors is the way they will take their work home with them. They can't leave the character they are playing behind them when they go away from the theatre or set. We'd got used to these strange transformations in our friend Meadows, which would take place a few days before rehearsals and last until long after the curtain had finally fallen or the camera stopped turning.

In the twenty years that we had known him we had enjoyed the polished charm of a *jeune premier* and the gallantry of a pre-war Polish officer, and suffered the grossness of a Mafia hit man, the stodginess of a CID inspector, the smarm of a Malamud KGB spy, and the greasy smoothness of a cigar-smoking tycoon. None of his roles made him into the ideal slave: the nearest he had got to gardening was playing the city-sickened exile in *Talking About Jerusalem*. And the nearest he had got to slaves was playing a Roman general in a television series.

But, strangely, his Roman General persona had a considerable impact on the garden. It made him intolerably imperious. He would boom about the house at weekends, dictating to everyone and almost making a slave out of me. Matters came to head when, with the match standing at 30-love in his favour in the final game, the last, balding tennis ball was lost.

'Time you got this bloody place cleared up, my boy. Nettles and lank grass everywhere—can never find the blasted ball.'

I found his angry thrashing through the undergrowth beyond the surround net to the south of the court infuriating.

It was *my* Dunlop racket which pinged and crashed every time he struck a stiff twig or a lurking rock.

Unsuccessful there, he swiped his way through the thick mattress of collapsing thistles and docks along the bank beside the barn. Somewhat reluctantly, he finally accepted a machette in exchange for the racket and set out to look for a ball lost earlier in the day between Fort Knox and Poet's Walk.

When he had finally settled for a drawn match and a glass of malt whisky, we both gazed round the areas he had trampled and laughed. Before his onslaught the weedy areas had at least looked natural. But as we peered at them the devastation seemed prodigious.

'Looks like a wheat field after a hectic chariot battle,' he chortled, still playing the Roman General.

'You're the expert,' I said, raising and draining my glass.

But although I had laughed it off I knew he was right. It doesn't matter whether it is interior decorating or gardening, the nearer a scheme comes to completion, the more the eyesores stick out. Lord Justice Mike—a stickler for order—had made similar remarks earlier in the summer but when I suggested that he should do something about it he had fled indoors.

There was no doubt that the garden would never look hospitable unless the few remaining wild areas were tamed.

Although I believe that, ideally, a garden should look like a watered glade in a Douanier Rousseau jungle, maintaining a convincing 'wild look' is very difficult. Nothing is more attractive than brute nature surging into life in spring. But after they have flowered, even the most entrancing weeds tend to collapse into an unexciting brown mass. And left to themselves they get thicker, and harder to penetrate, each season. The best wild gardens are the ones which receive the most attention. One of the nicest I've seen belonged to Hollis Barron, up among the giant redwood trees near San Jose in California.

But even with the slaves in the peak of mid season condition—their muscles finely tuned to hard work and their girths unhampered by excess fat—there was a limit to what they could accomplish. And I knew that a time would come when they would expect a weekend with us to consist of a little light weeding, some casual tennis, a read in the shade and a long walk. It was clear that whatever I planned for the rest of the garden, it would have to be something which, when finished, would require little maintenance.

Having shielded the north end of the tennis court with the Leylandii, we had planted a row of giant grass—Miscanthus sacchariflorus—at the other end to reinforce the Jerusalem artichokes. But since this grass—which, when fully grown, provides an attractive, dense, ten-foot-high windbreak—doesn't begin its flare of growth until quite late in the season, it seemed wise to plant beyond it something woodier and more persistent.

Rebellious and moody slaves who had downed tools and gone for a walk on Easter Friday in 1978 found the answer. A local wood, they said, was full of young seedling trees and bushes which seemed likely to die because the land had become boggy. Picking up their tools and dragging me with them, they went back to the wood and we dug out a couple of seedling horse chestnuts, three ash, two willows, a hazelnut and five wild redcurrant bushes.

I was doubtful whether they would survive since we were uprooting them at the beginning of summer. But there was plenty of rain until the week before harvest and they have all thrived to become what is known as Bushy Bank. The fact that we tried to take as much of the original root with the soil round it as possible (carrying the trees home in individual polythene rubbish bags) must have helped. So too would the liberal helping of peat we mixed with the soil in the deep planting holes.

Bushy Bank will look very handsome in a few years' time. And it cost nothing, save the price of the few grass plants and some effort. Saving woodland seedlings is not just a cheap way of thickening-up private gardens. Most of them would have been slashed down during the clearance of undergrowth which is part of the regular maintenance of a wood, and Britain, becoming a less leafy land, can barely afford such losses.

Approached politely most woodland owners would allow tree seedlings to be carefully removed. And many town gardeners would do well to copy the example of conservationists like Arthur Walker of Thornbury in Gloucestershire —he has rescued hundreds of trees which he has found pushing through the cracks between paving stones and walls or growing on demolition sites.

Much more work was required to dig out the deep-rooted nettles, docks, thistles, brambles and couch grass which had become set on the bank of the tennis court alongside the barn. Copying Terry's technique, I attacked it with the pickaxe and went so deep to search out the finest fragments of root that I loosened the soil dangerously. A good thunder shower would, I knew, badly erode the bank and have the posts of the surround net collapsing into the barn. I needed to quickly put up a physical barrier to soil movement and then to plant a tight carpet of topping vegetation to hold it permanently in place.

Happily, the operation coincided with the market launching of a new and quickly erected walling material which even a child can use. It comes in paving-stone-sized slabs (two feet square) which are made by setting ground Cotswold stone in cement. They are formed in such a way that they will fracture into six smaller (12ins by 8ins) slabs when thumped gently with a heavy hammer.

Since both flat surfaces are perfectly parallel, the pieces can simply be laid on top of one another to form a very stable wall without using any mortar to bind them. In two afternoons Doff and I effortlessly built an eighteen-inch wall along ten yards of the bottom of the bank, to hold back the soil. At various points along each course of slabs we left a gap between them to provide planting sites for alpine plants, and in the soil just behind the top of the wall we planted lamiums to provide foliage which would quickly tumble over the wall to soften the effect.

Although it all looked a bit new when we had finished, the broken edges of the slabs provided a fair resemblance to a traditional dry stone wall.

We took Beth Chatto's advice when planting the bank with five different species of highly decorative grass. They quickly established and will ultimately fuse to make a mad meadow producing a sequence of very attractive flower stalks.

To provide more vertical character to the area which we now call Grassy Bank, I popped in several shrubs including Senecio greyii (a silver-leafed evergreen with yellow daisies), a brace of buddleia to attract the butterflies, a winter jasmine for its early season blossoms, a Hebe and a sweet-smelling white-flowered Philadelphus. And these baby shrubs, which in future should develop into a perfumed and colourful jungle, had cost me practically nothing. They were the charming relics of one of my most successful gardening experiments—the propagation of shrubs from cuttings.

Taking six-inch cuttings from the tips of recently developed twigs on which the bark was still quite soft, I had snipped off most of the leaves and simply pushed the cuttings into a moist mixture of sand and peat in five-inch pots. To conserve moisture, the tops of the pots were covered with polythene bags. Kept out of doors in a sheltered place they had practically all rooted when I removed the bags after six weeks. I then put the pots in a sunny place to help the shrubs grow on. As a result of the morning's work I ended up with more young shrubs than I could use in the garden—although I found they made excellent birthday presents.

My only failure was with Leylandii cuttings which Mike Clift, Waterer's technical manager—who had urged me to use the propagation technique—said I should have taken in the autumn when the new wood was more mature. Otherwise my efforts met with complete success, a success which most gardeners, if they are prepared to wait a little for the final effect, could certainly emulate.

Having held back the soil on Grassy Bank the area below, right outside the east window of the barn, seemed very barren: a small patch of land, five yards long by three yards wide, it was in such a prominent position that it needed a little feature which, without a lot of attention, would always remain attractive.

Since the land was a very poor mixture of the hard core which had been used on the tennis court and rubble and clay dug out from the floor of the barn, I decided to create a completely synthetic growing bed. And in two days I had made what I call my 'micro-parterre'. It has turned out to be a splendid concept and one which would be most suitable for tiny areas like large sunny balconies or small town yards (provided that they are kept to be looked at and not for boisterous games).

I began by covering the whole area with a four-inch-deep layer of Drybrook crushed red-brown limestone, having

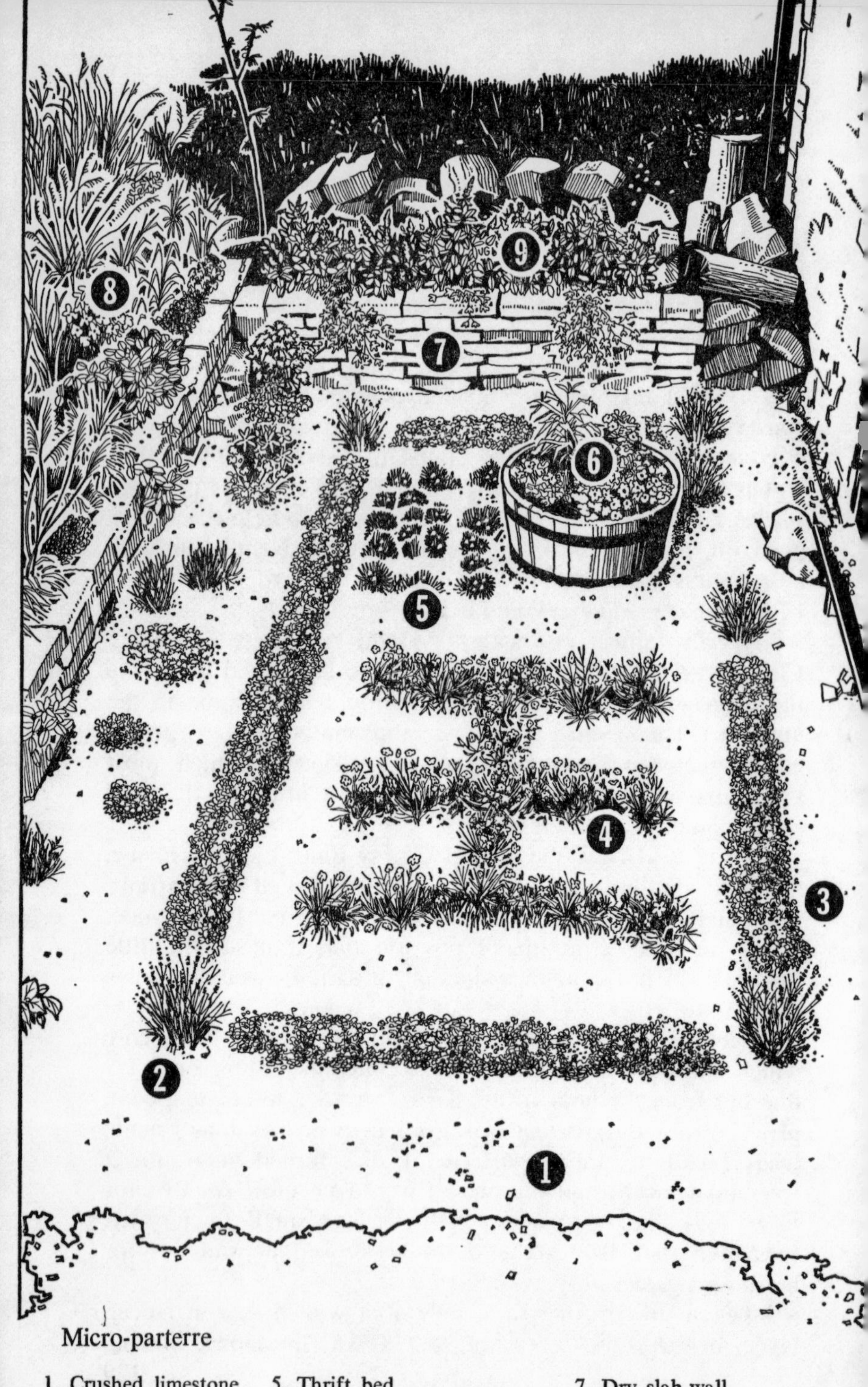

Micro-parterre

1. Crushed limestone
2. Lavender
3. Thymus aureus
4. Dianthus
5. Thrift bed
6. 24-inch tub with miniature bamboo, geraniums and petunias
7. Dry slab wall
8. Grassy Bank
9. Hebe variegata in raised bed

sprayed it with weedkiller. Using fragments of stone slab left over from walling the bank, I built a twelve-inch-high raised bed (twelve inches wide), half filled with old manure and soil mixed fifty/fifty, and topped with potting compost (John Innes No. 3), at the bottom of the plot. In this I set a line of container-grown evergreen Hebe variegata which have creamy green and white foliage and pale purple flowers and, at their feet to tumble down over the wall of the bed, three trailing ivies with finely chiselled small leaves. To make a pattern like a carpet border, I dug small planting pockets in the gravel, filled them with potting compost, and set in them pot-grown plants of dwarf, golden-leafed thyme. Their scented foliage will soon fuse in a continuous line. At the corners and in other strategic places along the line I planted tiny lavenders to provide horizontal features.

Offset from one edge of the rectangle—in the show-place just outside the barn window—I placed a large half-barrel tub filled with a mixture of soil and peat and topped with a six-inch layer of potting compost. As an all the year round feature I used a dwarf bamboo in a separate one-foot-diameter pot buried just to one side of the centre of the barrel. Surrounding that, I planted three rings of dazzling red little geraniums which left room for an outer ring of gay petunias to provide a flash of summer colour.

Beyond the tub I nestled white-and-pink-blossomed thrift plants into crushed stone to form a slightly asymmetrical carpet. In contrast, to occupy about one third of the north end of the rectangle, I laid out a spine of white-bloomed pinks escorted on each side by the spectacular pink called 'Sops in Wine' (Burgundy petals with white blotches). The straight lines trace out the letters 'HH' stuck together. I am still waiting for one of the more perceptive slaves to observe that it spells out the initials of the phenomenon which they christened —Hellish Holidays!

I was very uncertain what to do with the land north of Fort Knox, between the Lonicera hedge and the wall. The hedge was planted in the first year as a foil to the east wind and it became a rather dead area used as a passage—when it was passable. Its surface rose from south to north in a series of untidy hummocks which were difficult to mow. I thought that

Stepped terraces leading to the raised beds in Poet's Walk

1. Raised bed
2. Crushed limestone
3. Bamboo
4. Railway sleeper seat
5. Leylandii hedge
6. Lonicera hedge
7. Lilies in tub
8. Victoria plum
9. Poet's Walk

it was too narrow and insignificant to make much of a feature. I was quite wrong.

By cutting away at the soil on the high end—working as close as I could to the wall and trees on the east side and right up to the bottom of the Lonicera hedge on the west—I raked it down hill to raise the bottom level until the land was horizontal. Applying the same technique three times, I created three rough earth terraces.

To ensure that the final levels were really horizontal, I used the old Roman technique of comparing water levels at each end of a transparent hosepipe. It was taught to me by Terry when he laid the long canals for the water garden.

Edging the terraces with timber, I topped them with the same crushed limestone which I used to surface the micro-parterre.

When the terraces were finished, although irregularly shaped, they were surprisingly large. Most of them had a greater area than the rooms of many modern houses, and they now provide excellent sitting areas with a mixture of sun and shade.

Their construction taught me that even the tiniest, most awkward pieces of land have some potential—and indeed such areas are often more spacious than they initially appear.

Since our garden lacked lilies, the terraces provided an excellent opportunity to plant some in tubs to mark the steps.

When the terraces were complete, they looked so tidy that the tall Leylandii hedge nearby seemed very bedraggled. It obviously needed topping and trimming. This would have been a tricky task without another invaluable tip from Terry.

Although the individual trees were nearly twelve feet high their stems were still relatively thin and fragile. An ordinary ladder leaned against them would undoubtedly have snapped many branches. But a six-foot wooden plank across the top of the ladder spread the load across several trees. Although there were anxious moments as it settled when I made the first ascent, this simple device enabled me to trim the top of the hedge easily, quickly and much more cheaply than from the complicated steel scaffold arrangement which I was planning to buy.

By the end of 1978, there only remained the problem of what to do with Poet's Walk. When the oak tree and the hedge were in full leaf it became very shady and intolerably dry, a very difficult combination for a gardener to deal with.

Back in 1973, after a visit to the famous Exbury Gardens near Southampton, I had planted £30-worth of beautiful young rhododendron plants in that area. They had never really prospered. Rabbits attacked them unmercifully. They were always under stress from lack of water and supplying it with a hose attracted moles which did their best to uproot them. Finally, the droughts of 1976 and 1977 killed off the last of them.

Ironically the vicious frosts of early 1979, in consolation, provided a superb rosy pink flowered Drama Girl Camellia to begin the re-establishment of that area.

One evening in early February my colleague Gwen Nuttall and her husband were disturbed by a noise in the garden when dining at their charming Stockwell home. Suspecting brigands they ran out still with fork in hand. They didn't find anyone, but they did notice that the far side of the garden wasn't as dark as usual. Gwen, with the same intrepid attitude which strikes such fear into the hearts of City chairmen, ran across the lawn. She discovered that twenty feet of beautiful old brick wall had collapsed because of the frost—all over one of the best sections of her border.

The impact was more devastating than a collapse in the stockmarket or an increase in the price of red wine. But with true Northern spunk she choked back her tears, began picking up the bricks and the next day kindly offered me the sound but giddily leaning Drama Girl Camellia. It had to be moved, she explained, because no one could rebuild the wall with the shrubs in place.

Within twenty-four hours of being moved, Drama Girl had been placed in the sheltered areas of broken shade at the foot of the elm totems at the bottom of Poet's Walk. To go with it Giles Trehane, who runs a nursery near Wimborne in Dorset, which specializes in shade-loving plants, suggested several plants which we could grow in the dry soil at the foot of the hedge because they would tolerate both dry and shady conditions.

However, he made it clear that if only there was more moisture available in the soil, there was a wonderful range of shade-loving plants which could be used to provide much more colour and interest. Sadly, he was asking for conditions which didn't prevail, and I had more or less resigned myself to the fact that Poet's Walk should remain merely a nice leafy and secluded area enlivened by those plants which would tolerate dry conditions.

But then James Dyson rang. I had met him several years earlier and been impressed by his boyish enthusiasm and the brilliance of his designs. At the time he was launching his Ball Barrow which, with its fat inflated ball in place of a wheel, permits massive loads to be moved easily over wet and rough ground.

He wanted to see me, he said, to explain one of his latest gardening inventions—a very cheap form of irrigation. And, as he exposed the simplicity of a valve which when snapped into an ordinary half-inch garden hose line would regulate the flow of water to numerous capillary watering pipes, I realized that he had solved the problem in Poet's Walk. By running a hose underground from the bottom of the cattle-shed to the top of the area, I could take off as many branches as I liked at little expense and provide water at many points at the turn of a single tap. The system would enable me to grow many of those moisture- and shade-loving plants which Trehane had mentioned. It would also support several of the exquisite dwarf rhododendrons and azaleas which I had coveted on a visit to the Edinburgh Botanical Gardens.

Since the whole area was underlain by the thirsty roots of the oak and damson trees and the hawthorns of the hedge, simply supplying water to the soil at their feet would have helped them prosper but not have guaranteed the survival of anything which we planted.

So I decided to create nine one-foot-high raised beds—six along the margins of Poet's Walk and three on the terraces—to make a new environment for plants. Each bed would be filled with a mixture of fine, moisture-retaining, ground Forest Bark and peat. This would ensure that most of the water I applied would be used by my plants and not by the trees and shrubs of the hedge.

But a problem I had overlooked was that of providing walls for the raised beds. The existing stone wall on the east side of the walk would act as a backing for three of the proposed beds; but that still left 160 feet of wall to construct.

Making such a length of wall in stone or brick would take a long time. As always, I was impatient. An easy and very satisfactory solution, I knew, would have been to make the walls from peat blocks. They would certainly look wonderful —much softer and more natural than brick or stone, and their surfaces would turn beautiful green and brown as mosses and lichens established themselves.

The problem was the expense. Even buying the peat blocks in bulk they would cost more than £120. Since the whole irrigation system for more than 70 feet of bed averaging over 18 inches wide (including an overall main run of 120 yards) would only cost £25, the price of peat blocks seemed excessive.

The final solution was appealingly simple. Robert Green was slowly, as his seasonal farming activities allowed, taking down all the elms on his land which had been killed by Dutch Elm disease. Since most of their timber was of too low a grade for making furniture, he was cutting it into two-and-a-half-feet lengths which were then split down into sections averaging eighteen inches at their widest point. He kindly let me have enough of these logs to create palisade walls for our raised beds. Having pushed one end of the logs into a narrow trench, I then nailed the tops on to a simple frame made up of 3ins by 2ins of rough timber. When filled the beds looked splendidly natural, and it seemed pleasantly appropriate to use timber from trees which had grown and died in the district to create a whole new growing environment. Almost poetic in fact.

Chapter Eighteen

The dreadful reality didn't actually strike me until I realized that I couldn't shut the kitchen door. All those hired gilt chairs had overflowed from the hall of our flat in London and blocked the doorway. Things had come to a sad pass. Even my loving but habitually sleeping family, in the rooms along the corridor, had ganged up against me in preparing the celebrations for my fiftieth birthday.

Since I couldn't close the door I was even deprived of the solace of Anthony Parkin taking a rural breakfast during his *On Your Farm* radio programme (you can usually hear the cup clinking if you concentrate). Early morning radio was forbidden in our house unless the kitchen door was closed, so I just sat drinking my first half-pint of coffee and smoking cigarettes.

It was pointless getting depressed. For days I'd been telling myself that one birthday was just like another and that there was nothing important about reaching the half century. But because the family in its kindness intended to mark the event with a bumper banquet at home, I couldn't just ignore it.

There was no point in trying to shrug it off with a gay, 'Splendid—I've reached the halfway mark.' I knew damn well that I was at least two thirds gone. After all the delicious pâté and the sauce Béarnaise it was probably nearer three-quarters. It was a dreadful thought. I had hardly made up my mind about how to earn my living. So many possibilities had already disappeared.

My claim to fame as an entomologist had never been recognized. The geoapterigimeter (a device for heating soil constructed by placing my mother's dustbin on three bricks and lighting a gas ring below) had failed completely. Designed while I was still at university, this brilliantly conceived piece of equipment would, I hoped, warm the soil sufficiently to make the wingless insect denizens bolt to the surface to be collected, identified and counted—'a priceless aid to anyone doing a soil survey'. Sadly, although many insects did emerge, a scrape below the surface revealed an even greater number of well-cooked earthworms, millipedes and leather-jackets.

Neither that apparatus, nor the papers which I had written with the late John Britten for an international aviation conference in the 1950s about the behaviour of liquid droplets thrown out of aeroplanes, had won me a Nobel prize.

My impudently early book on crop protection had failed to gain me a university chair—and, even more surprising, no one had bought the film rights. The MCC had never called to enquire, after a flawless forty-one not out and some late cuts and leg glances as glorious as anything David Gower could produce, whether I would be available for the tour of Australia. The Walker Cup team selectors had never responded to my thumping 290-yard drives and fine rounds on the Old Course at St Andrews. Worst of all, my hair was fast disappearing and I would never have one of those fine middle-aged heads which are graced by silver-grey sideburns.

Perhaps my depression was profounder because, as a second-crop newly-wed, I'd been able to ignore the trauma of reaching forty in the excitement of a new life. Whatever the reason for this mood, it did enable me to review my life from a different angle.

Clearly, the past fifty years had been a dismal failure. My talents had never been recognized. Even the thing which I thought I was best at and which I enjoyed most—gardening—had produced no more than niggardly rewards.

Take for example the tennis court. The martialled, balletic boredom of lessons at school had turned Doff off the game. But in Canada and America she had become a keen badminton addict. Just before we got married she had said casually, 'I'd like to learn to play tennis properly before I reach forty.' And, prompted by that sentiment, soon after buying the house I had raced off to see the man who was enlarging the car park at the pub.

At the time a decent hard court would have cost approximately £2,500. Since basically it was only a car park with a slightly posher top (with some absolutely vital loose fine tarry grit to permit the feet to glide) I was correct in assuming that a regular tarmac car park contractor would be able to do the job. So that for £800 for the finished surface I was well pleased. Happily, at the time a new heavy-grade rigid plastic netting was just starting to be produced. Attached to wires strung between ten-foot lengths of angle iron sunk two feet into concrete, it provided an excellent surround for another £90. Wonderful plastic white line tape hammered into the tarmac with nails (an easy but back-breaking task) and £50 for posts and a net finished the job.

Well, it wasn't quite Wimbledon and it has collapsed a little in places over the years, but anyone accurate and clever enough to hit the critical undulations deserves to win the point. And given more time to do the land levelling myself and the availability of 'ready-to-use' tarmac products, I could probably still do the job for a similar price today.

But was it to be worth it, I wondered on the glum birthday morning. All the slaves had fought for the chance to play on the court the day Henriette and I finally nailed down the lines. That was a long time ago. Doff, whose present it was, thought it was lovely, but she was always far too busy in the house or the garden to become enmeshed in such a long game. After their initial spate of enthusiasm it always seemed to be too hot, too cold, or too windy for the slaves to play.

So that in my fiftieth year the court had been used for a total of one hour and twenty-five minutes. Meanwhile it took up more than 2,500 square feet of garden. That was land which could have become an enchanting sunken rose bed or even just hard standing for containerized shrubs, I thought bitterly.

Still, thanks to the slaves, most of the heavy work in the garden had been completed. Perhaps in future I might spend some time on the court—work up my backhand and whirlwind service? Too old, of course, for serious stuff, but perhaps there would be a niche for me at veteran level—my Latin master always thought I was quite promising.

By the time the second cup of coffee had worked its way through to my liver I had begun to view the court in a better light. Even if it wasn't used often, it was a nice asset. And just creating a court for so little outlay was quite an achievement.

The eight o'clock news cheered me up too. Even without me, the England cricket team was doing well in Australia, and, when shuffled out of the kitchen by determined women an hour later, most of my depression had vanished. Any lingering regrets I might have had about the passage of time were swept away by the delicious aroma of fine food emanating from the kitchen.

The Black and Decker electric saw sent by my mother was a wonderful surprise, as was the weathervane and camera presented by Doff and Liesi. But I was a bit disappointed when, after a lavish meal, Faber hadn't brought me anything. He just gave me, on behalf of all the slaves, a card with their good wishes and said that they had done 'a little something to the garden with Mike Tucker's help'.

Trying to appear grateful, I was worried. I had heard queer ideas for improvement expressed from time to time and didn't relish the thought that some of them had been implemented.

Although it was late by the time everyone had left, I was up early the next day, feeling wonderful. Fifty and a bit seemed far more acceptable than the round half-century, particularly as the sky was clear and all the fields glistened under a hard frost when I sped down the M4 to find out what the slaves had done.

Although impatient to discover their folly, when I climbed out of the car I was so impressed by the winter beauty that I was momentarily distracted. Forgetting what the slaves had done, I admired the results of my own labours. I had deliberately tried to create conditions which would provide winter beauty. And it had worked really well.

Frost crystallizing on mummified foliage and moribund flowers can provide some of the garden's most spectacular and magical effects. By planning ahead in spring, summer and autumn, a green-fingered necrophile can ensure a glittering winter-plant mausoleum to greatly enhance the garden during the dead months.

Round the perimeter of the garden, where plant forms tend to be profiled against the horizon, great restraint is needed.

After an early spring or late winter pruning of hedges and a trimming back of weeds and grasses at ground level, everything should be left to prosper. Vines—like wild hops, honeysuckle, old man's beard or even deadly nightshade—should be encouraged to track through the summer twigs to provide a knotted hoary tracery in winter. And the haws of hawthorn or the hips of dog roses, allowed to flower unhindered, will enliven grey days with bright red beacons which flash like pearls when frosted. Below, relict flower stems of wild grasses like cocksfoot, or the inverted parasol framework of dead cow parsley, which are lost among the general froth of foliage in summer, stand out like sentinels in winter.

Despite the fact that hard frosts had bitten back many of the plants in herbaceous beds it was astonishing how, in more fortunate corners, a few flowers of calendula, nicotiana, dahlia and michaelmas daisy had escaped destruction and still hung on to display encouraging points of colour. Not the most sensational plants, their value lies in the pleasure they provide late in the season.

Looking at the remaining dahlias, I could imagine the horrified reaction of those experts who always pinch out terminal buds to obtain fewer but bigger blooms. Disgusted by the current mania for larger and more garish flowers, we heretics always allow our dahlias the liberty to bloom as they please—the smaller blooms which they produce are much more enchanting.

The roar of Concorde overhead distracted my attention and reminded me of the purpose of my mission. So I strolled round the garden trying to decide what the slaves had done.

It was obvious that there had been no major earthworks. However, when I began to examine particular areas more critically, there were telling changes. In the shubberies at the bottom of the lawn, fine bush roses had been planted, a line of smaller roses had been arranged as a short hedge across the top end of the long herbaceous bed. Five tiny miniature roses stood marginally higher than the leaves of the pinks in the bed alongside the main water canal. Three more bush roses reinforced the Queen Elizabeths in the raised bed at the side of the paved court.

It was a charming gift, thoughtful and highly imaginative. And it would help to put the slaves' final stamp on a garden which they had been largely responsible for creating.

It struck me that all gardens reflect the attitudes and temperaments of their creators. Martialled lines of tulips or dahlias in scrupulously weeded beds betray the retired military man more surely than his burnished shoes. A jungle of weeds struggling to camouflage a shocking abstract sculpture, hints at the happy Bohemian and piles of unwashed dishes by the sink. Tiny corners, like cages for exotic birds, in which foliage and flowers rampage to provide a constant tapestry of wonderfully blended colour suggest a gentle nature. Looked at that way our garden was hard to categorize. It was an amalgam of many ideas and embodied the personalities of everyone who had helped to make it.

Greatly moved (or rather 'full' as we would say in the North) I paused just outside the gate and gazed all round the property trying to remember the wilderness which it had been when I had first looked at it with Martyn nearly eight years before. Even in the barrenness of winter that desolation was difficult to recall.

We had pushed back the wilderness. It had been replaced by most of the traditional elements of an English garden. Apart from tidying up a few small corners and replacing unsatisfactory plants with others, there wasn't much left to do.

We had sufficient herbaceous border to keep the slaves in weeding whenever they felt like bending their backs. More than enough lawn to tax the engine of even our giant mower. Flowering shrubs and ornamental trees were becoming sufficiently mature to make an impact on the landscape.

There were terraces, secluded shady areas and sunny spots; walls festooned with climbers and hedges permeated with ramblers. The espaliered peach and fig were shaping well and the apples had yielded their first diffident crop. There was even an extensive water feature and, of course, when my birthday gifts flowered, there would be roses absolutely everywhere. I had no doubt that, despite their occasional awkwardness and intransigence, they had been a decent bunch of slaves.

Still pondering, I heard the scrape of boots on the hard track behind me and looked round to see an almost unrecognizable version of Sneer. He was even more bedraggled than ever and, like me, looked older than at our first meeting. But instead of his habitually sour look he greeted me with a radiant grin.

'I see you did it then—took my advice in the end.'

Realizing that I couldn't understand what he meant, he pointed up the side of the hedge which had been destroyed by Dutch Elm disease. At first I noticed nothing exceptional, just the bramble canes which had been woven among the dead elm twigs and had thickened into fine protective pillows, climbing from the ground to over eight feet high.

'Nothing like them species roses for spreading in a hedge,' he said, decisively pulling the remnants of what must have been an undertaker's overcoat more closely about him and beginning to move away.

I still didn't understand. Nor did I understand when his grin disappeared and he shouted loudly, 'Come by, you little sod.' But as I looked down I realized that the order was addressed to a new dog—an eager little Jack Russell which was busily sniffing round the wheels of my car. Thankfully there was no sign of his sly mongrel.

'He looks a good one,' I said admiringly to Sneer as he walked away.

'Ah mate, he'll be the one to 'ave your rabbits,' he shouted back over his shoulder.

Curious about what he had said about the hedge, I went back through the gate to have a look.

Sneer had been much more observant than me. Every eighteen inches from the point where the dead elm began, right to the top of the garden, a rose had been planted at the foot of the hedge. Their labels told me that many of them were Rugosas—the traditional old British briar rose found wild in many hedgerows. Others were tough, fast-growing shrub roses like those planted to form the hedge at the bottom of the garden.

When I had examined the labels to a point beyond the greengage tree, I began to understand the magnanimity of the slaves' offering. Walking slowly right down the full length of the garden I carefully counted the number of roses which they had had planted.

Reaching the bottom hedge I suddenly realized the significance of the figure. There were exactly fifty. Fifty roses, for a man called Rose on his fiftieth birthday. I didn't know whether to laugh or cry. But since no one was looking I did snivel a bit before unlocking the house to telephone my thanks.

I was tingling with the warmth and depth of their friendship as I drove back to London, thinking about the wonderful way the roses would rampage through the hedge to spike its pinky-white bramble blossoms with a pageant of other colours and reinforce it as a shield against the wind.

But I hadn't reached the motorway junction at Shefford Woodlands before I was assailed by a very worrying thought.

On the previous evening, when the claret and Grand Marnier had begun to do their work and loosen tongues, I had been privy to three troubling confidences. Director Cox's Sara told me that they had just bought a flat in Kensington 'and we get the garden with it, so you will have to tell us what to do'. She had a look of bright expectancy.

A little later, in philosophical mood, Faber admitted that he was becoming fed up with living in town and was 'seriously thinking of buying a place near Newbury with three-quarters of an acre of land'.

Di, too, looked pleased when recounting that Lord Justice Mike's books and papers had taken up so much space in their flat that they were just about to exchange contracts on a house in Hampstead 'with a big patch of garden which could be lovely'.

Remembering what they said as I swung on to the M4 I muttered aloud, 'Thank God Meadows has emigrated to France.' Because it suddenly struck me that if I wasn't very careful, I too could become a slave.

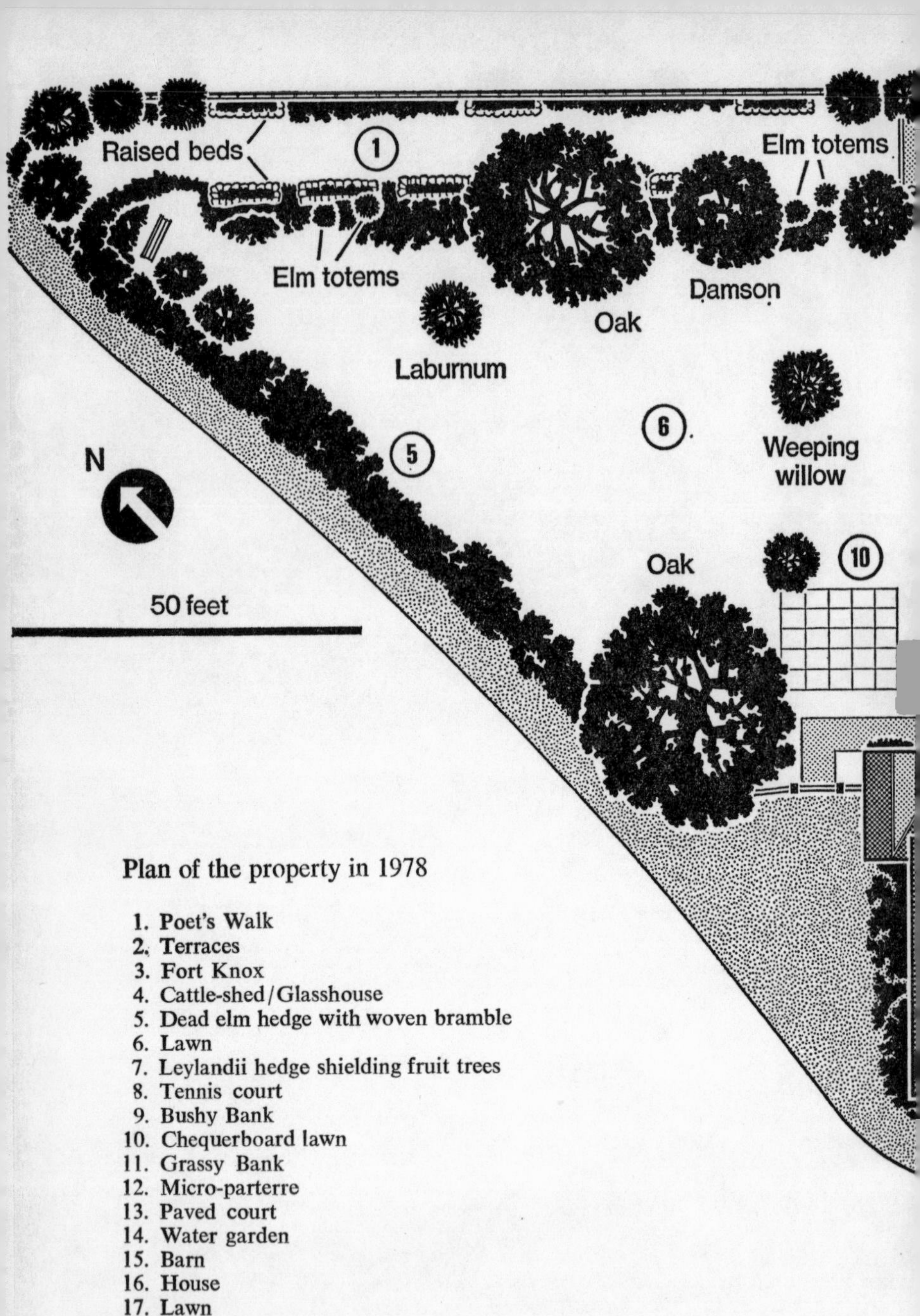

Plan of the property in 1978

1. Poet's Walk
2. Terraces
3. Fort Knox
4. Cattle-shed / Glasshouse
5. Dead elm hedge with woven bramble
6. Lawn
7. Leylandii hedge shielding fruit trees
8. Tennis court
9. Bushy Bank
10. Chequerboard lawn
11. Grassy Bank
12. Micro-parterre
13. Paved court
14. Water garden
15. Barn
16. House
17. Lawn

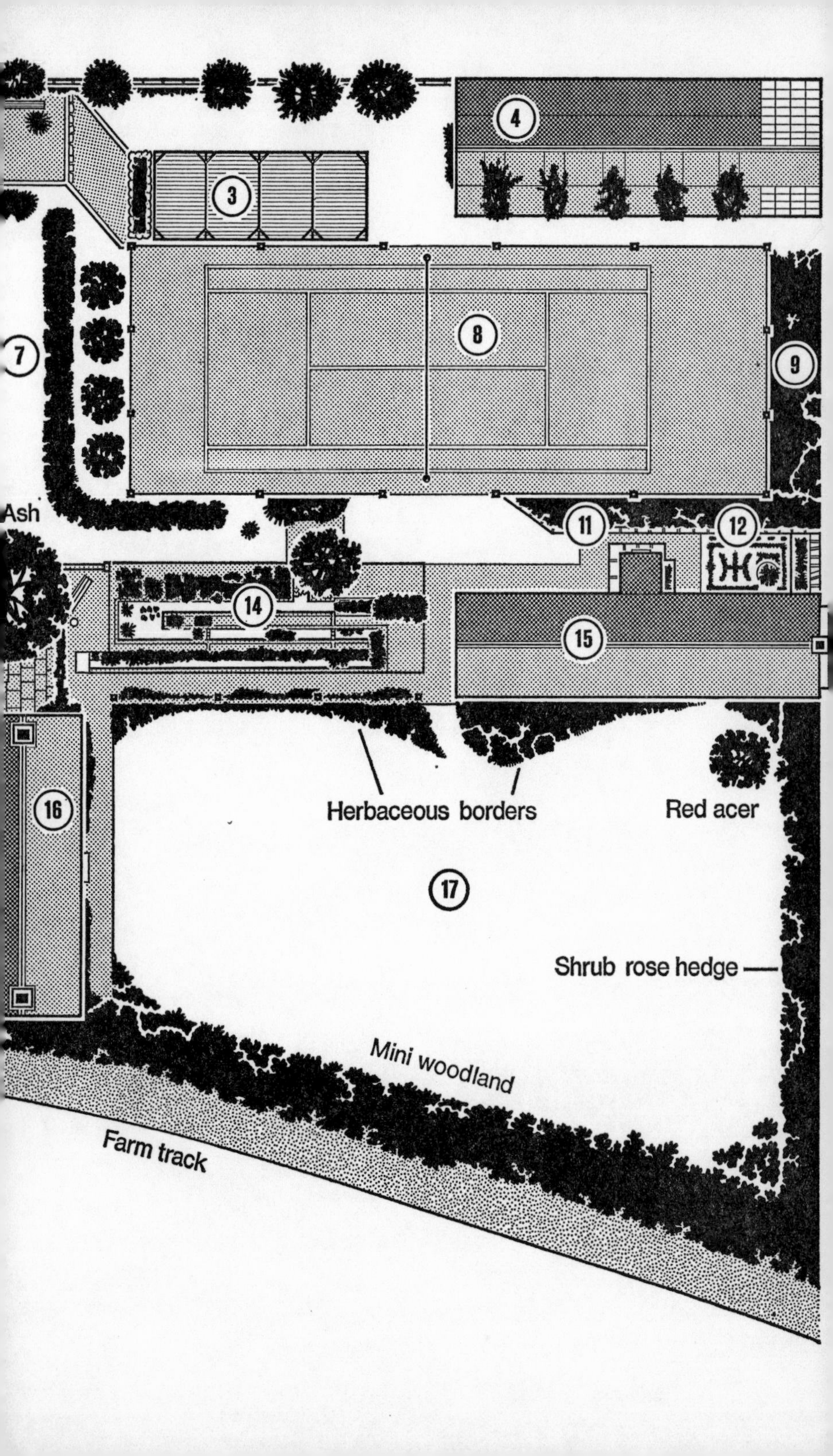

4
3
7
8
9
Ash
11
12
14
15
16
Herbaceous borders
Red acer
17
Shrub rose hedge
Mini woodland
Farm track